From Military Rule
to Liberal Democracy
in Argentina

About the Book and Editors

Argentina has most of the characteristics that various theories of democracy postulate as prerequisites for achieving liberal democracy: an urban industrial economy, key economic resources under domestic control, the absence of a peasantry, the absence of ethnic or religious cleavages, relatively high levels of education, strong interest groups, and well-established political parties. Yet for most of the post-Depression period, the country has been ruled by nondemocratic regimes. As a result of the current process of democratization, however, a liberal-democratic political culture is emerging. The question is whether this process, which is strongly supported by all political parties and interest groups, can be consolidated in a context characterized by economic stagnation (and, in the past decade, retrogression), an inflation rate at the three-digit mark, growing unemployment, and the third-largest foreign debt in Latin America.

This collection of essays focuses on economic, political, and cultural aspects of the transition from military rule to liberal democracy in Argentina. Contributors discuss the factors leading to the demise of the military regime established in 1976, the electoral victory of the Radical Party in the 1983 elections, the most critical issues facing the Alfonsín administration, and the prospects for the institutionalization of democracy.

Monica Peralta-Ramos is in charge of academic affairs at the Argentine Embassy in Washington. **Carlos H. Waisman** is an associate professor of sociology at the University of California, San Diego.

From Military Rule
to Liberal Democracy
in Argentina

edited by Monica Peralta-Ramos
and Carlos H. Waisman

Westview Press / Boulder and London

Westview Special Studies on Latin America and the Caribbean

This Westview softcover edition is printed on acid-free paper and bound in softcovers that carry the highest rating of the National Association of State Textbook Administrators, in consultation with the Association of American Publishers and the Book Manufacturers' Institute.

Published in 1987 in the United States of America by Westview Press, Inc.; Frederick A. Praeger, Publisher; 5500 Central Avenue, Boulder, Colorado 80301

Library of Congress Cataloging-in-Publication Data
From military rule to liberal democracy in Argentina.
  (Westview special studies on Latin America and the
Caribbean)
  Includes index.
  1. Argentina—Politics and government—1955–   .
2. Argentina—Economic conditions—1945–   .
3. Argentina—Social conditions—1945–   .
I. Waisman, Carlos H. (Carlos Horacio), 1943–   .
II. Peralta-Ramos, Monica.
F2849.2.F69 1987   982'.06   86-4068
ISBN 0-8133-7101-5

Composition for this book was created by conversion of the editors' computer tapes.
This book was produced without formal editing by the publisher.

Printed and bound in the United States of America

The paper used in this publication meets the requirements of the American National Standard for Permanence of Paper for Printed Library Materials Z39.48-1984.

6   5   4   3   2   1

Contents

Tables

Introduction

This volume brings together the papers presented at a conference on the transition from military rule to liberal democracy in Argentina, held at the University of California, San Diego, on February 3–4, 1984.

Transitions to democracy took place in several South American countries in the early eighties, but the Argentine case is especially significant, for two reasons. First, the previous military regime was much more repressive in this country than in the other nations of the sub-continent in which democratic regimes were recently established (Bolivia, Brazil, Uruguay). Second, conditions in Argentina are especially inauspicious for the legitimation of a high-participation competitive regime: the economy is stagnant and prospects for growth are bleak in the face of a foreign debt equal to over five years of exports; further, the institutional bases of authoritarianism—in particular, armed forces and a security apparatus imperfectly controlled by the government, powerful interest groups and weak political parties—is still in place.

The papers in this collection discuss economic, political, and cultural aspects of the transition, from different disciplinary perspectives and theoretical orientations. Taken together, these analyses present an awesome inventory of obstacles to the democratic transformation of the country. The authors focus on issues such as the combination of a structural economic crisis and an unpayable debt, the pattern of destructive conflict among different segments of the capitalist class, the decay of manufacturing and the expansion of the informal sector of the economy, a political culture based on a tradition of elite-led movements that control the subordinate classes, the need for the new democratic government to attain minimally satisfactory outcomes in all the major issues it faces, a culture ambivalent about capitalist values and national identity, the legacy of a culture of fear which corrupted large sectors of the society, even the rejection of science and technology, and the decline of the creative and critical potential of the intelligentsia.

And yet the radical nature of the crisis is in itself an element of hope for the consolidation of liberal democracy. The appearance of guerrillas and of state terror in the seventies were extreme manifestations of the crisis of legitimacy in which Argentina lived for decades, whose consequence was the institutionalization of violence as the standard mechanism for conflict resolution. Because the situation was so extreme, non-democratic formulae and their carriers lost their legitimacy, and this includes not just the militaristic groups on the far left, but also the armed forces, the economic and political elites that supported authoritarian options, and the trade-unionists prone to corporatism. At the darkest point in Argentine history since the organization of the national state, a military regime practiced, in the name of life, liberty, property, and religious values, the abduction, torture, and killing of real and imagined opponents, the confiscation of their property, and even large-scale corruption. At the end of such a regime, Alfonsín and the Radical Party won elections by promising little more than a return to the rule of law, a government guided by the principles of conventional morality, and an equitable assignment of the burdens of reconstruction.

Herein lies the strength, as well as the weakness, of the Alfonsín administration. The different groups in Argentine society see the current attempt to restore democracy as the last chance to avoid chaos. This definition of the situation may help produce permanent changes in Argentine political culture and contribute to the institutionalization of pluralism, autonomous participation, moderation, and bargaining. However, politics at the edge of the abyss is never a good thing: if the new government does not fulfill to a minimum degree the modest expectations of the citizenry, the outcome will be the de-legitimation of the last road not taken, high-participation liberal democracy, and the intensification of the crisis to an unprecedented scale.

* * *

The first set of papers focuses on the relationship between politics and the social and economic structure. David Rock's "Political Movements in Argentina: A Sketch from Past and Present" has a deceiving title. This article is more than an outline of the origins, organization and consequences of the political movements that have been a central feature of modern Argentine history, Yrigoyenism and Peronism in particular. It is an interpretation of Argentine politics, according to which the "movement" type of political organization, rooted in the Hispanic past and in Catholic doctrine, is the institutionalized pattern of interaction between elites and subordinate classes in Argentine society. This explains the impulse, in some segments of the now ruling Radical Party, toward multi-class coalitions and populist policies. It follows from this analysis that the consolidation of liberal democracy, whose mechanism for the organization of political inputs is the party rather than the movement, would require changes in deeply ingrained aspects of Argentine political culture.

Michael Monteón's "Can Argentina's Democracy Survive Economic Disaster?" discusses the economic situation the Alfonsín government encountered when it came to power at the end of 1983—stagnation, hyper-inflation, and a staggering debt. The paper traces the origins of this situation: Argentina's structural crisis, caused by the country's position in the international economy, and the disastrous economic policies implemented by the military regime established in 1976. The paper shows the inadequacy of the Alfonsín administration's indecisive and populist response to the economic crisis during the first year and a half, and it provides an excellent background for the understanding of the shift toward "stabilizing policies" (the Austral Plan) in mid-1985. These policies have reduced inflation, but the government has done little, so far, to restructure the Argentine economy and make growth possible again. The options in relation to the debt are still hotly debated, and Monteón's argument that repudiation need not be an unmitigated disaster runs counter to the conventional view, which equates default with chaos.

Monica Peralta-Ramos's paper, "Toward an Analysis of the Structural Basis of Coercion in Argentina: The Behavior of the Major Fractions of the Bourgeoisie, 1976–1983," deals with the social process leading to hyper-inflation in the seventies and eighties. She shows how, in the conflict over the distribution of the surplus, different fractions of industrial, financial, and agrarian capital resorted to speculative strategies in order to advance their interests and impose their demands. Hyper-inflation was one of the symptoms of this cleavage, which led to the deterioration of institutional mechanisms and ultimately to the decline of the legitimacy of the political system and of the social order in general. The paper analyzes this conflict during the Peronist administration of 1973–1976, and especially during the subsequent military regime, and reveals its role in the collapse of both. It follows from this argument that the survival of liberal democracy requires not just economic growth, but also a drastic re-organization of Argentine capitalism.

Juan M. Villarreal's contribution, "Changes in Argentine Society: The Heritage of the Dictatorship," claims that the most important determinant of the anti-industrial policies carried out by the military regime was not economic but political: these policies aimed at weakening labor and the segment of the industrial bourgeoisie that supported Peronism. The attempt was successful, and the relation of forces in Argentine society has definitively changed. The paper shows how the working class diminished in size and also in social and political weight, and it proposes that, in the new stage, white collar employees and other non-proletarian sectors will be the central subordinate political forces. Thus, Argentina finds itself in a paradoxical situation: the country, which never was a mature industrial society, failed to develop the party system that is typical in that type of society; and yet it is making a transition of sorts to a backward type of post-industrial society. How will post-industrial politics look in a society with a large and impoverished state apparatus, an expanding informal sector, and large and frustrated professional, student, and intellectual strata? This is a true leap in the dark.

Finally, Carlos H. Waisman's paper, "The Legitimation of Democracy Under Adverse Conditions," discusses both the factors that hinder and the ones that contribute to the process of democratization. The negative factors are three: the economic crisis, the fact that the institutional basis of authoritarianism and corporatism (a partially autonomous state apparatus, strong interest groups, and weak parties) is still in place, and the weakness of liberal-democratic traditions. The favorable factors are: the de-legitimation of non-democratic formulae as a consequence of their failure, and the commitment by the Alfonsín administration to institutionalize the two dimensions of democracy, participation as well as contestation. These favorable factors may lose their efficacy as the different social and political forces pursue their interests in the context of the acute economic crisis. The success of the transition to democracy entails two processes: the weakening of the institutional infrastructure mentioned above, and the display of at least a modest degree of efficacy by the new political institutions. The first of these processes requires the effective subordination of the military and the security apparatus to the government and, especially, the transformation of Peronism into a party of democratic opposition. The second process, finally, presupposes some economic growth, and this in turn entails a need for industrial reconversion.

The second group of papers deals with the relationship between politics and culture. Juan E. Corradi's "The Culture of Fear in Civil Society" examines the effects of the widespread terror practiced by the recent military regime on social and cultural life. This piece contains Corradi's comments and conclusions about the papers contributed to a seminar on the subject. Three issues are particularly important: first, the discussion of how individuals who are the object of intimidation by a terrorist state respond, by either adapting or, less likely, by resisting governmental pressures; second, the analysis of the semantics of fear, in which official discourse focuses on a spurious opposition between "violence" and "order," that masks the underlying affinity between the two; and third, the description of the functioning of literary and journalistic life in contexts of institutionalized fear.

Julie M. Taylor's "Technocracy and National Identity: Attitudes Toward Economic Policy" explores the cultural dimension of the intense abhorrence, in current Argentina, for the pseudo "free market" economic policies carried out by the Martínez de Hoz team in the late seventies. In Taylor's view, the strength of this opposition reveals, in addition to the explicit economic and political reasons, the deep ambivalence that exists in the country's culture about technical or universalistic values, and ultimately about Argentine identity. These economic policies were defined as the manifestation of capitalist and foreign interests, in a nation whose members doubt as to whether they belong to the first or to the third worlds; at the same time, the members of the Martínez de Hoz team were perceived as "the best and the brightest," and thus the failure of their policies could be interpreted as the failure of the Argentines.

Hector J. Sussmann's "Culture, Ideology, and Science" poses the question of the country's scientific backwardness. This is not a trivial issue, given the fact that Argentine levels of development, standards of living, and enrollments in higher education were, in the first half of the century, higher than in much of Europe. He finds an answer in the cultural sphere, rather than in economic and political factors. From 1870 to World War II, Argentina was transformed by mass immigration, the development of agriculture and of industry, urbanization, the expansion of education, and the extension and decay of liberal democracy, but these changes failed to destroy, he argues, the traditional Hispanic antagonism to science and technology. He documents this hostility under different political regimes (oligarchic, Peronist, military) and brings up the contrasting example of Japan, a country which, being less developed than Argentina until the beginning of the century, strove hard to acquire foreign science and technology.

Finally, Noé Jitrik's "Elements for an Analysis of Argentine Culture" contains provocative observations about the deterioration of Argentine culture, not only as the result of the repressive policies applied in 1976–1983, but also as a consequence of the conceptions and practices of different intellectual and political groups in the period preceding the military regime. He stresses the complicity of sectors of the official establishment and the political intelligentsia in the adoption of policies that deepened the cultural crisis and rendered it chronic. Repression under the military aggravated this situation, by impairing the creative and critical capacities of Argentine society, and by producing a form of culture based on counter-values such as repression, self-censorship, and vigilance.

* * *

Some of the papers were revised and completed during 1985. In addition to these authors, other participants at the conference were Mirta Botzman, Aaron Cicourel, David Collier, Ruth Collier, Jaime Concha, Emilio De Ippola, Benjamin F. Hadis, Tulio Halperin-Donghi,

Tim McDaniel, and Miguel Murmis. The conference was supported by the Organization of American States and by three units at the University of California, San Diego: the Chancellor's Associates, the Center for Iberian and Latin American Studies (CILAS), and the Third College. Publication of the papers was made possible by a grant from CILAS. In particular, we acknowledge the support and encouragement given to the project by the late Roberto Etchepareborda, of the Department of Cultural Affairs of the OAS; Michael P. Monteón and Paul W. Drake, directors of CILAS; and Faustina Solís, Provost of Third College. Mary Cooper and Carolyn A. Morrissey translated the chapters by Villarreal and by Jitrik and Peralta-Ramos, respectively. Elizabeth Burford typed the manuscript with her usual efficiency and cheerfulness.

Monica Peralta-Ramos
Carlos H. Waisman

PART ONE

Politics, the Economy, and Society

1

Political Movements in Argentina: A Sketch from Past and Present

David Rock

In late January 1984 *La Prensa* reported on the newly elected Alfonsín government's plan to create a National Forum of Workers (*Encuentro Nacional de Trabajadores*). The exact form and functions of this body—indeed whether it was any more than just an idea—remained uncertain. But it was widely understood the new government intended to make a determined bid for trade union backing: faced by an enormous foreign debt and by a domestic recession it could hope at best to mitigate but could scarcely avoid, the regime had to act fast to broaden and consolidate its support. The National Forum thus marked the inception of an effort to coopt or divide Peronism, and as the recession deepened to prevent the Peronists from mobilizing a mass working class opposition. Among members of the government memories were still fresh of the events of 1963–1966. At that time a Peronist trade union "Battle Plan" (*Plan de Lucha*)—mass strikes, street demonstrations, and civil disobedience—had paved the way for a military coup and the downfall of the last Radical constitutional government led by Arturo Illia.

La Prensa, however, regarded the *Encuentro Nacional* as something more than a mere political tactic, inspired by the lesson of past errors. It interpreted the proposal as signaling the metamorphosis of *Alfonsinismo* from its base in the Radical Party, (the *Unión Cívica Radical*), into a "movement," drawing its support from much broader political forces. *La Prensa* also predicted that this movement would be launched by exploiting the deep-rooted popular antimilitarism that stemmed from "*la guerra sucia*" of the late 1970s. *La Prensa* understood a "movement" to imply a form of populist corporatism. "*Movimientismo,*" it declared, is a response to "crisis," and also a transitional political order "while democracy is maturing"; it is typical of a "political culture like the

Argentine, which has always been based on highly developed integrative movements," (*se ha asentado siempre en el integrismo "movimientista" más absoluto*); an integrative movement means a "society divided up into 'branches' (*ramas*)—of business persons (*empresarios*), trade unions, political groups, women's groups, and even organizations of children and old people."[1]

No doubt *La Prensa*'s speculations invite some immediate criticisms. Political conditions in Argentina in early 1984 were such that the new constitutional government was shaky from its very beginnings. The regime had to make immediate and energetic efforts to protect itself: increase its support if it could, and continually outmaneuver a strong opposition. Under the circumstances it was quite conceivable that the Alfonsín government might try to utilize the lingering aftershock of extreme military repression to deflect public attention away from current issues, among them hyper-inflation and falling standards of living. But it was difficult to envisage the government permanently buttressing its support on such an emotional and therefore potentially fragile foundation. We might suspect that a better tactic would be to exploit the foreign debt issue, and to attempt to sublimate internal tensions in a nationalist campaign against foreign banks or the international financial institutions.

Secondly, the reference to the "*ramas*" illustrates *La Prensa*'s well-known paranoia at anything remotely reminiscent of political conditions during the early 1950s. When the Perón regime of 1946–1955 found itself in growing economic and political difficulties after 1948, it began tightening restrictions on the press. The inveterately anti-Peronist *La Prensa* refused to comply with the censorship. In 1951 the government banished its proprietors and confiscated the newspaper. Soon after Perón sought to impose a tighter and less arbitrary system of political controls, generically defined in Peronist propaganda as "The Organized Community" (*la comunidad organizada*). Under this plan numerous new corporate associations, entitled *uniones, confederaciones,* or *ramas* were formed within the Peronist movement. They each represented such groups as business, the professional classes, women, university and high-school students, and they were additions to a similar type of organization among trade unions and the urban working class. The regime gave these associations equal standing with one another, intending them as vehicles to articulate and process political demands from different sectors. However, the *ramas* were assembled in such a way under authoritarian Peronist bosses so as to filter and limit such demands. The system also obliged groups seeking government responsiveness to their sectional demands to enter into a relationship of formal subordination. Thus the *ramas* would help strengthen the regime's authority, and also cushion it against pressures from other corporate associations outside the Peronist movement it had found difficult or impossible to control.

In the event *la comunidad organizada* was never fully consummated, and the tensions the effort to implement it provoked played a major part in Perón's overthrow in September 1955. Yet in this period Argentina came closest to developing into a full-fledged fascist state. *La Prensa* remembers Peronism during this era as the highest exemplar of *movimientismo*, an experience it remains desperately anxious to avoid repeating.[2]

The obvious error here is to make an exception into the general rule, an aberration into the norm. Proto-totalitarianism along the lines of "The Organized Community" is a possible *dénouement* of *movimientismo*, but one neither necessary nor pre-ordained. Yet aside from any specific objections we may make against *La Prensa*'s assessment, its analysis also mirrors some classic and illuminating studies in comparative politics that have examined the movements in numerous locations, both in Latin America and beyond.[3] *La Prensa* is also correct to view the movements, or *"movimientismo"*, as among the most ubiquitous features of twentieth century Argentine politics: were *Alfonsinismo* to evolve in this form, it would be scarcely setting any precedents. Two great examples of *movimientismo* overshadow twentieth century Argentine political history: Radicalism or *Yrigoyenismo*, and the parent of *Alfonsinismo* on one hand; *Peronismo* on the other. But besides them are numerous other less important movements, some no more than putative, amounting to little more than plans, adventures, or aspirations.

The *Liga Patriótica Argentina*, formed in early 1919, acquired some of the traits of a movement on a campaign of nativism, anti-Semitism, and anti-Communism.[4] During the 1920s *Lencinismo* and *Cantonismo*, both of them offshoots of Radicalism, were examples of movements within provinces.[5] After the 1920s came many other local movements like them: Amadeo Sabbatini's neo-*Yrigoyenismo* in Córdoba during the 1930s and early 1940s, Manuel Fresco's organization in the province of Buenos Aires before its destruction by President Roberto M. Ortiz in 1940,[6] and the neo-*Peronismo* of Felipe Sapag in modern Neuquén. *Uriburismo* of 1930–1931 was an early example of an intended movement that failed.[7] In more recent times the examples are almost endless. *Movimientismo* was among the cardinal features of Arturo Frondizi's various political organizations. Such features germinated during Frondizi's early association with the nationalistic Radical party pressure group, the FORJA, during the late 1930s. They reappeared during Frondizi's government between 1958 and 1962, and they survived in the small splinter party Frondizi has led since 1962, the Movement for Integration and Development (MID).[8] *Movimientista* aspirations of a more authoritarian brand were apparent in the corporatist projects of the Onganía regime of 1966–1970.[9] Former president Pedro E. Aramburu was reportedly plotting to launch a popular movement through his UDELPA party immediately before his kidnap and death in 1970. The *Gran Acuerdo Nacional* created by President Alejandro A. Lanusse in 1971–1973 was designed to draw the political parties into a coalition to legitimize Lanusse's rule through elections. Much of the strategy of the Montonero guerrillas after 1970 was based on a search for popular support to convert a clandestine band into a mass movement. Finally, *movimientismo* reappeared once more in the competing populist projects of military leaders—Massera, Viola, Galtieri—in 1979–1982. Since 1955 a score or more political leaders, both civilian and military, have engaged in abortive attempts to spark popular movements to carry them into power.

Movimientismo: Some General Features

Movements are usually erected upon *caudillos,* and often exemplify the peculiarly Latin American politico-cultural tradition known as "personalism." Movements confer leadership on individuals, whose ideas and personalities are believed to embody a set of general interests or goals. The following citation from Eva Perón's *La razón de mi vida* shows, using typically sexual and semi-religious imagery, that leaders of movements claim power that is charismatic, sacred, transcendental and authoritarian. Perón, his wife proclaimed:

> is a giant condor flying high and sure among the clouds close to God. Had he not descended to me and taught me to fly, I could never have beholden the marvelous and magnificent immensity of my people. And therefore neither my life nor my heart belong to me, and nothing of what I am is my own. All that I am, all that I have, all that I think, and all that I feel is Perón's.[10]

Thirty years before Hipólito Yrigoyen claimed a similar authority that also rested upon a symbolic fusion between himself and his supporters. In the eyes of his supporters Yrigoyen incarnated the popular will, and in this guise he became a human metaphor of patriotism. *La Epoca,* the leading metropolitan *Yrigoyenista* press organ before 1930, issued the following description of the street procession led by Yrigoyen in May 1919 to commemorate the revolution against Spanish rule. The assembled onlookers, *La Epoca* reported:

let forth a deafening hosanna of triumph and redemption, a mixture of prayer and thunder, solemn and reverberating, to the great patrician (i.e. Yrigoyen), in whose manly form the flag is made human. . . . The multitude paid reverence to the great statesman . . . . It said to him breast to breast, heart to heart, that he had acquitted himself well with his country. He was their president, their great president, a star among the thousands of small components of this universe . . . . As he passed, the multitude encountered a mirror and a symbol of itself. As he passed by, it granted him an apotheosis.[11]

Movements that have acquired any cohesive form, as opposed to transitory or spontaneous demonstrations like the *cordobazo* of May 1969, have never sprung from below. Elites manufacture movements. Among the chief functions of the movements is to create routes to power for elites. Alternatively elites employ movements as defense barriers to check opposition. Movements are also instruments to effect radical changes in public policy. Thus the formation of Radicalism in the early 1890s has been interpreted as a response among segments of the landed gentry to its exclusion from government; in a search for power, this gentry forged a mass base, using the demand for popular democracy as the agent of mobilization.[12] In a similar way Perón has been frequently depicted as the leader of a military elite of economic nationalists that emerged during the early 1940s. The military nationalists espoused an independent, and also anti-American foreign policy, and a program of autarky and industrialization. When opposition threatened to derail such policies in 1943–1946, Perón organized the trade unions and the urban working class as instruments of countervailing pressure. Afterwards, during the later 1940s, Perón's movement provided the political backing for a program of industrial development.

The movement constantly seeks to transcend class or sectional divisions. In aiming for consubstantiation with the community at large, or claiming they represent a higher interest than that of faction or segment, movements seek to enhance their legitimacy. Thus in 1909 Yrigoyen defined his nascent movement as "not a party in the conventional sense . . . but a conjunction of forces arising from national opinion."[13] The movement, he declared, welcomes support from any "legitimate interest . . . its bosom nurtures all the elements that sincerely wish to offer themselves in the service of the country's true welfare."[14] Despite its initial close alignment with urban workers, Peronism too soon developed similar aggregative, inclusive pretensions. Among the "Twenty Truths of *Justicialismo*" issued in October 1950 were the following: "Peronism is essentially popular. . . . Only one class of men exists in the eyes of Peronism: he who works. . . . For every Peronist there is a single scale of values: first the Nation (*La Patria*), then the Movement . . . and then men themselves."[15] In a similar vein in September 1983, Raúl Alfonsín described his party as a "great movement—national, popular, democratic, committed to change" (*transformador*).[16]

Movements represent a willingness to use state power actively and forcefully promote a "harmony of classes." In *Yrigoyenismo* class harmony meant "distributive justice" (*justicia distributiva*), a commitment that quickly established tensions between the movement's doctrines and the prevailing liberal individualism of the period. Thus under Yrigoyen Radical Party propagandists were wont to claim that "excessive capitalist privileges (had) disappeared. . . . (Trade unions) have ceased to be treated by the State as hives of anti-social outcasts. They have become a living part of Argentine society, worthy of being listened to, and the claims they represent met."[17] Under Peronism "social justice" had the same essential meaning: bringing a hitherto politically excluded or disenfranchised class under the protection of a paternalist state. In both cases "justice" was also a necessary precondition of political stability, which implied too that in justice lay the key to political legitimacy. Thus in a speech in August 1945 Perón declared that: "the solution (to our problems) is to bring social justice to the masses. . . . We must organize popular groups, and through them uphold the stability (*equilibrio*) of the State."[18]

As movements claim to represent the Nation, they also purport to defend the nation against alien enemies. Indeed invoking some external threat, real or imagined, and proclaiming the need for self-defense against it, represents one of the most common tactics adopted by movements to forge a sense of common identity and unity. Movements crystallize as a means to resist "foreign" or "un-Argentine" ideologies. Anti-Communism, for example, had a major role in the gestation of numerous right-wing nationalist movements before 1945. In 1944–1945 Perón invoked alleged Communist penetration to justify his concessions to the urban working class, and his support for state-controlled trade unions. Later, under General Juan Carlos Onganía, Communist infiltration became one of the chief justifications for the 1966 coup d'etat. Diffuse brands of anti-imperialism have often served much the same purpose as anti-Communism. In the late 1920s *Yrigoyenismo* derived much of its popular *élan* from the campaign to nationalize oil, and eliminate American oil interests. In the 1946 election Perón skillfully persuaded the electorate that the choice before it was "Braden or Perón": the latter's brand of popular nationalism, or surrender to United States business imperialism symbolized by former ambassador Spruille Braden. The leftist guerrilla movements of the 1970s exploited antipathies against monopolistic foreign corporations. General Galtieri's attempt to reimpose

Argentine rule in the Falkland Islands in 1982 was another attempt to fashion a popular base, or deflect popular opposition, on a wave of anti-imperialist sentiment.

Movements aim to establish pyramidal communication linkages between their elites and their popular base in such a way as to bureaucratize the authority of their leaders. Such links serve as propaganda channels, and as means to exchange benefits or rewards from above with active support and endorsement from below. Under *Yrigoyenismo* the pyramid took the form of an interlocking hierarchy of party committees (*comités*) that stretched from Yrigoyen himself into the smallest sub-precinct of the cities or the remotest hamlet of the countryside. Dominated by local bosses, known in the cities as *caudillos de barrio*, the committees were often petty microcosms of "personalism," the bosses trafficking in patronage in the form of jobs, recommendations or informal welfare assistance in return for electoral support.[19] Peronism developed similar features. The movement was explicitly "vertical" in structure. Perón maintained control over the working class through a hierarchy of unions supervised by the CGT. In Peronism the same general functions as the Radical *comités* were performed by "basic units" (*unidades básicas*). As the activities of the Eva Perón Foundation showed, both before and after the death of its patroness, Peronism too sought to exploit personal services and organized charity for political purposes on an even greater scale than the Radicals.

The 1970s provide contrasting examples of the same general techniques among factions or political leaders of widely differing ideological orientations. In 1972 the conservative Francisco Manrique sought to carve a political base in the north-western provinces by personal handouts of food and other articles among small farmers and peasants. Almost simultaneously, the most radical of the guerrilla groups then active, the *Ejército Revolucionario del Pueblo* (ERP) demanded ransoms in the form of free distributions of foodstuffs in the shantytowns of Córdoba for the release of kidnapped executives of multinational companies. In the mid-1970s José López Rega used the Ministry of Labor and Welfare as a gigantic patronage machine, and instigated President Isabel Perón into resurrecting the style of daily charity-work used twenty five years before by Eva Perón. Still more recently in early 1982 Galtieri organized a sequence of government-sponsored public barbecues in some of the provinces. Such events, which punning Lanusse's *Gran Acuerdo Nacional* ten years before critics dubbed the "*Gran Asado Nacional*," were widely recognized as the prelude to an attempt by Galtieri to launch a popular movement.[20]

To agree once more with *La Prensa*'s analysis, "crisis"—the collapse or derailment of some hitherto functional scheme of social and political development—is the most common underlying spur to the formation of movements. Before 1950 crises in Argentina were largely *conjunctural*: they were temporary shocks, usually external in origin, but which eventually passed. From the late 1940s crisis became *structural*: permanent, embedded, inescapable. The distinction helps to illustrate the growing frequency of *movimientista* attempts during the past thirty years, and to indicate why more recent movements have continually failed. Both *Yrigoyenismo* and *Peronismo* took power during the conjunctural crises of world war. However, both movements consolidated themselves during periods of recovery and relative reequilibrium after the wars, when their leaders had access to the material resources to strengthen the alliances that had carried them into power. More recently structural crisis has continually erected incipient movements but simultaneously deprived their sponsors of any opportunity to institutionalize their popular followings.

The birth of the *Unión Cívica*—the forerunner of Radicalism in 1890—provides a classic illustration of the role of crisis in the gestation of movements. This improvised coalition of politically displaced elites, alienated catholic groups, and second-rank urban politicians like Leandro N. Alem, sprang from financial collapse in opposition to the Juárez Celman government. The *Unión Cívica* exemplified some of the classic traits of *movimientismo*: displaced elites using popular mobilization in the effort to gain power, and employing incipient anti-imperialism as a mode of bridging class divisions.[21]

Yrigoyenista Radicalism had some of the general features of the movement from its inception during the late 1890s, when Yrigoyen took over control from Alem. Yrigoyen's aloof and secretive style suggested an implicit claim for charismatic authority. *Yrigoyenista* propaganda was invariably vague and unspecific. Its moralistic, diffuse tone was deliberately constructed to enable the party to transcend regional and class cleavages. Thus *Yrigoyenista* discourse referred to Radicalism simply as "the Cause," infallibly destined to supersede its oligarchic adversary, "the Regime": Radicalism had an "apostolic mission" to restore the Constitution, implant democracy, and realize national unity. Yet the maturing of Radicalism as a movement was largely a consequence of the severe class frictions of 1918–1919. Under severe attack from the military-backed *Liga Patriótica* in 1919, Yrigoyen adopted "personalism." He rapidly increased state spending, using his control over public funds to strengthen his middle class popular support. At this point the Radical *comités* became the main instruments to link the state with the electorate through a burgeoning spoils and patronage system.[22]

Analogous crisis conditions underlay transitions in the form and development of Peronism. Perón's movement first appeared during World

War II. In the early 1940s Argentina lost its established grain markets in continental Europe; the subsequent change and contraction in the rural sector prompted mass migration from the country into Buenos Aires. Besides suffering severe economic and social tensions, throughout the war Argentina faced diplomatic conflict with the United States, as the latter struggled to force Argentina into a role of client state. Out of such internal and external conflicts came the military coup of 1943, and then an effort to industrialize led by the nationalist military; Peronism, with its large working class base, emerged as the political instrument through which to pursue industrialization.[23]

Yet Peronism too underwent renewed evolution after the economic crisis of 1949. During its first years in power before 1949 Peronism was essentially a labor party: the government taxed farmers to create urban jobs and increase urban wages and living standards. However, with the collapse of the post-war boom and the advent of the balance of payments "bottleneck," Peronism swiftly transformed itself into an adjudicatory regime. The government used a variety of techniques—incomes policy, "verticality," charismatic leadership styles, and finally "The Organized Community"—in an effort to strike a balance between leading socio-political groups whose relations with each other grew increasingly competitive.[24]

Movimientismo: Some Historical Roots

The movements belong mainly to the twentieth century, to a society of large cities, highly developed social structures, and to the era of mass communications. Yet their roots are to be found in the country's beginnings as a Spanish colonial dependency. Some of the salient ideological components of *movimientismo* spring from Roman Catholic doctrines that can be traced as far back as Aristotle. In stressing the ethical and mediatory functions of political power, Catholicism provided the ideological buttress for such precepts as the duty of the state to promote "harmony," for "distributive" or "social" justice, and for the patriarchal relationship between elites and masses the movements epitomize. Many such ideas also contain bastardized residuals of medievalism—the mutual responsibilities of lord and vassal, the existence of a divine-inspired hierarchy.

Catholic political doctrine, first introduced to Latin America during the sixteenth century, underwent refurbishment and modernization during the late nineteenth century in an effort to counter class conflict ideology arising from European industrialism. From this late nineteenth century restatement, twentieth century proponents of *movimientismo* obtained much of their vocabulary and rhetoric. The following quotation is taken from the papal encyclical *Rerum Novarum* of 1881. Its precepts recurred almost verbatim on numerous occasions in *Yrigoyenista* or *Peronista* propaganda:

> The great mistake (is to assume) that class is naturally hostile to class, and that the wealthy and the workingmen are intended by nature to live in mutual conflict. So irrational and false is this view, that the direct contrary is the truth. Just as the symmetry of the human frame is the resultant of the disposition of the bodily members, so in a State is it ordained by nature that these two classes should dwell in harmony and agreement, and should, as it were, groove into one another, so as to maintain the balance of the body politic.[25]

Yet Catholicism is not the only influence on *movimientismo* that derives from Argentina's Hispanic past. The Spanish colonial system was erected vertically and patriarchally upon a material base that comprised forced tribute expropriations by the white minority from subject non-white peoples. From its beginnings, and except among the white elites themselves, the colonial system was inherently inimical to political associations along horizontal lines that grouped the subject peoples. Spanish colonialism thus established patterns in which political activism became legitimate among elites alone. Elites themselves could seek wider support among subject peoples for their own particular purposes. But any spontaneous or independent politicization beyond the elites invariably provoked energetic efforts to suppress it.

The early colonial history of the River Plate region provides several examples of this elitist political tradition in the making. Soon after the creation of the city of Santa Fe in 1573, local mestizos organized a successful uprising against the handful of whites who controlled the community. The chief goal of the rebellion was to achieve equality of civic status between whites and mestizos, giving the latter the same legal claim as the whites to local resources of wild cattle, horses, or captured and enslaved Indians. But the movement was swiftly quashed by outside intervention. Subsequently, Santa Fe and the other Spanish cities of the region adopted ordinances rigorously excluding mestizos from full civic status, and subordinating them to the whites. Another similar episode occurred during the Calchaquí rebellion of the 1650s, a rising of the Diaguita Indians in present-day La Rioja. The movement was instigated by a Spanish renegade, Pedro Bohórquez, but its main purpose was to achieve exemptions from Spanish tribute. With the rebellion at its height Spanish militias invaded the valley. Having quickly subdued the rebels, the Spaniards enslaved the survivors, distributing them among the cities in the surrounding governorships.[26]

On the other hand, the colonial period contains numerous examples of elites mobilizing subject peoples on their own behalf, most commonly for military purposes at times of intra-elite conflict. One such case was the *"comunero"* war of the early 1730s between the Spaniards of Corrientes and Asunción on one side and the Jesuit missions of the Upper Paraná on the other. Conflict between them stemmed from competition in the trade in yerba mate—the staple product of both regions. The settlers also wanted access to the large, and in their eyes, underutilized Indian labor pool concentrated in the missions. For decades the settlers had sought to achieve their objectives by pressurizing the authorities in Buenos Aires, Lima, and Madrid. Eventually, however, having been constantly outmaneuvered by the Jesuits, the settlers adopted *"comunerismo,"* a form of radical local chauvinism, and an ideology that enabled them to claim that the resources and economic advantages they sought were theirs by right of citizens' privilege and entitlement. Upon such claims the *comuneros* launched their movement, and led their Indian and mestizo retinues into a devastating attack against the missions.[27]

Politics in Buenos Aires in 1806–1810 provides perhaps the best documented example to illustrate the continuities between forms of popular political mobilization in the colonial period and those in the twentieth century. Late colonial society in Buenos Aires differed from the standard Spanish American model in that an Indian population, and therefore tribute institutions, were virtually non-existent. However, the city had a substantial black population, composed of both slaves and freedmen, and a diverse ethnic base—conditions that enabled Buenos Aires to reproduce the broad stratification patterns and the elitist political forms typical of the Spanish empire elsewhere. In 1806 the British invasion of Buenos Aires destroyed the small regular imperial garrison, and irreparably damaged the imperial administration. Following the invasion, and its similarly abortive successor in 1807, a power struggle erupted among a *mélange* of competing elites; amidst such instability developed another precursor of *movimientismo*.

The "movement" here consisted of the popular militia established to replace the imperial garrison, and repel the British. The militia resembled a modern movement in that it emerged in response to "crisis." It also became a means to create vertical linkages, and a sense of social solidarity, that spanned ethnic and functional divisions within the community. Like a twentieth century movement, the militia became the political instrument of one alliance of elites—the creole "patriots" who in 1810 led the city into revolution and the struggle for independence— in their struggle for dominance against other elites—those supporting unreformed ties with Spain. The militia offered an early example of the state deploying its powers of reward and patronage to promote a species of "social harmony." Anyone remaining outside the militia stood at the mercy of economic disruption and inflation caused by the Napoleonic wars and the collapse of foreign commerce. However, to be inside the militia meant cooptation by the State, and admission to the perquisites and protection of public employment.[28]

Still another anticipation of twentieth century movements was *caudillismo*, the regionally based political system that emerged from the collapse of central authority during the independence and civil wars. *Caudillismo* was another example of crisis-generated hierarchical authoritarianism, in which the *caudillos* themselves claimed charismatic authority emanating from their military prowess and their successes in defending their provinces from anarchy or from destruction by outsiders. Such features were visible in *Rosismo*. Rosas was an outcome of crisis. He achieved power in Buenos Aires in 1829 in the aftermath of the disastrous war with Brazil, the near-collapse of the cattle-exporting economy, civil war and government bankruptcy. For more than twenty years Rosas employed symbolism and populism to buttress his authority, constantly invoking the external threat from his "unitarist" enemies to justify his resort to dictatorial power.[29]

After Rosas a national state displaced the regional order represented by *caudillismo*. Rapid economic growth swept aside most of the remaining residues of the colonial order. Several million European immigrants transformed the country's ethnic composition. Yet amidst such revolutionary change, it was also remarkable how much of the past survived; among the survivals perhaps the most pronounced lay in political forms. Thanks basically to an unchanged land tenure system that enabled the old elites to become the main beneficiaries of economic expansion, a modified patriarchalism flourished during the late nineteenth century under the national oligarchy. With the political pacification that followed national unity in the early 1860s, elites gradually ceased having to recruit support by forming armed bands of supporters. However, the *personalismo* of this period, in which politics remained dominated by elite factions, and functioned around personalities of preeminent social status or exceptional political skills, was often little other than a form of demilitarized *caudillismo*. In much the same way as the *caudillos* had distributed booty from their conquests, the oligarchic factions created and maintained their political bases through personal rewards and offices. Throughout the late nineteenth century the older warlike rules or the newer peaceful rules of political conflict oscillated one against the other according to circumstances: if a peaceful contest failed to achieve victory, resort would be made to war and revolution. In Buenos Aires in 1874, 1880 and 1890, for example, factions that had first tried to win power through elections, immediately afterwards turned to rebellion as the alternative. Only as the rebellions recurrently failed did their incidence decline, though as twentieth century politics has so frequently shown, the tradition of armed revolution was never completely expunged.

In 1912 Argentina adopted the secret ballot and universal male suffrage for native and naturalized Argentines. Sponsors of the Sáenz Peña reform claimed that liberal democracy marked the completion and consummation of a revolutionary modernizing process set in motion by economic and social development two generations before. In the event, however, the 1912 reform achieved little beyond still further evolution and readaptation from within the original patriarchal mold: "personalism" simply acquired a more democratic and populist guise. Radicalism, for example, the chief beneficiary of the electoral reform, proclaimed by Yrigoyen the embodiment of the new democracy, never completely abandoned the right it had claimed in the early 1890s, which it also inherited from an earlier nineteenth century political tradition, to resort to insurrection and revolution. Yrigoyen's position of informal but supreme command in the party bore unmistakable resemblances to that of the nineteenth century *caudillos*. Like the "personalist" oligarchs Yrigoyen claimed to have superseded, he too eventually trafficked in patronage, office, regards and favors. These were among the features that prompted the famous Socialist Party critique of Radicalism: the party was an atavism of "creole politics" (*política criolla*), personalist and paternalist, behind all its rhetoric to the contrary formless and unprincipled, capable only of responding to circumstances or pressures rather than seizing the initiative and actively shaping reform policies. In a similar way another unfriendly critic, Lisandro De la Torre, dubbed Radicalism "a hybrid conglomeration, that moves like a snake on the thrust from its tail."[30]

Post-1955 Movements: Stymied Resurrections

Both *Yrigoyenismo* and *Peronismo* were products of social change, and new political expressions of emergent social classes; the former of the large new middle class bred by a maturing export economy, the latter of an urban proletariat fashioned by migration and industrial diversification. The strength and longevity of both movements thus stemmed from their leaders' success at latching onto new social groups, offering them enfranchisement and access to the material rewards of power. Under Yrigoyen the diffusion of benefits to the middle classes mainly took the form of an expansion of the state as an employer, or widening the channels of social mobility through measures like the University Reform of 1918. With Perón a similar distribution of benefits was accomplished by increasing the wage share of national income, and through a program of social reform.

Both Yrigoyen and Perón implemented such redistributive measures, initially at least, during periods of rapid economic growth. Most of the resources for their programs thus came from an economic largesse generated by exports rather than from transfers or appropriations from other social sectors. Yrigoyen, for example, lurched into "personalism" during the post-war trade boom of 1919–1921: his government increased spending largely by virtue of growing revenues from trade. Likewise, the post-war boom of 1946–1948 enabled Perón to tax farmers and farm exporters through the IAPI, then to deploy the revenues to expand industrial jobs and wages, and to erect a new trade union movement under government control.

Both Yrigoyen and Perón, however, eventually found themselves facing recession, which meant that continuing redistribution could be upheld only either by inflationary measures, or through inter-sectoral transfers. Under these conditions both faced increasing, and ultimately unmanageable, political tensions. When they attempted to halt redistribution, they alienated their own supporters, and their movements began to splinter; alternatively, if they continued redistribution, they provoked united opposition from among the groups or sectors they were taking resources from. Yrigoyen first confronted this dilemma during the post-war depression of 1921–1922, as exporters and big business began to demand cuts in state spending to curb growing public indebtedness. Conflicts between the business advocates of low spending and the middle class supporters of higher spending played a major part in the division of Radicalism in 1924 into an *Yrigoyenista* populist wing and an "anti-personalist" conservative faction. Finally in 1929–1930, at the onset of the world depression, similar tensions had a central part in Yrigoyen's downfall by military coup d'etat.

Under Perón similar conditions emerged after 1948, as export earnings fell and industry became increasingly stagnant. From 1949 politics became a delicate matter of balancing the demands of one sector against those of others. Perón proved stronger and more resourceful in dealing with such issues than Yrigoyen. But he was unable to surmount them, and they underlay his fall in September 1955.[31]

Conditions since 1955 provide multiple examples of convergent pressures at once creating and reproducing movements, but also constantly destroying them. On one side chronic crisis arising from economic stagnation, from inflation and political deadlock, continually provoked political elites, both civilian and military, into bids for mass support. However, the persistence of crisis also prevented the elites from institutionalizing and consolidating their followings: movements were thus recurrently strangled either at birth or in early infancy. Moreover, unlike Radicalism after 1900 or Peronism in the mid-1940s, the post-1955 movements were rarely directed at newly forming social sectors emerging from broader, long term change and development. Instead their targets were already constituted groups with well-defined, entrenched political loyalties. Since 1955 each essay into *movimientismo* has been aimed at enlisting the Peronist working class, frequently with the explicit intent to create a "Peronism without Perón." Until Perón's death in 1974 the failure of such efforts was explicable simply enough as a result of resourceful and successful resistance from Perón himself. Also while Perón remained alive, his supporters continued to believe he would eventually return to power—a belief that was ultimately vindicated by events.

But even without Perón himself barring the way, one wonders whether any *movimientista* project after 1955 could have successfully united a society increasingly fragmented by inflation and by the violent short-term changes affecting the Argentine economy. The classic illustration of the alternating forces that continually spur the formation of movements but almost simultaneously destroy them occurred during the Peronist restoration of 1973–1976. When Perón reassumed the presidency in late 1973 with more than 60 percent of the popular vote, many believed that his movement would remain in power for a prolonged and indefinite period. In the event, scarcely six months later by the time of Perón's death in mid-1974, his popular alliance had already begun to disintegrate. Afterwards Perón's designated heirs led by Isabel Perón proved totally incapable of holding the coalition together. In 1975 the movement fragmented at an accelerating rate, and within eighteen months was virtually defunct.

No doubt the speed of the collapse was due in some measure to political mismanagement under Isabel Perón. But had Perón himself lived, it seems likely that even he could at best have slowed the disintegration rather than have halted it completely. The new Peronist movement of the mid-1970s brought together, under a facade of unity created by Perón's skilled tactical maneuvering, a wide variety of social sectors and political factions with many conflicting expectations, programs, and interests. Perón hoped to continue binding them together through a "Social Pact" between unions and business that established a prices and incomes policy. The Pact succeeded in doing this during the brief economic boom of 1973–1974. But it swiftly collapsed in the aftermath of the Arab-Israeli war of 1973, when rapidly rising oil prices turned the international terms of trade drastically against non-oil primary producers. Following the oil crisis, costs of imported goods required by local industry leapt upwards. Manufacturers could no longer observe the price freeze. But as domestic prices rose, demands for wage increases quickly followed. Soon after the Social Pact, and the aspiration for an institutionalized class alliance it represented, disintegrated in a wave of inflation. As inflation then swept out of control, support for Isabel Perón ebbed away. The economic crisis was not the only source of the acute political instability of the mid-1970s. But there seemed little doubt that had the economy remained stable, the Peronist restoration would have enjoyed a far greater chance of success.[32]

In the mid-1980s *movimientismo* thus remains as central a feature of Argentine politics as ever before. No doubt efforts to erect new movements will continue. But in the absence of the broad conditions that enabled *Yrigoyenismo* and *Peronismo* to develop as durable political vehicles of emergent social classes, the movements seem destined to rise and decline with the same frequency as during the past thirty years. *Movimientismo* is a manifestation of a political culture rooted in Hispanic colonization. Today, as an almost continual process of creation and decay, it is also an epiphenomenon of a crisis Argentina continually proves unable to surmount.

Notes

1. *La Prensa* (Buenos Aires) 28 January 1984.

2. For a longer discussion of *La Comunidad Organizada* see my *Argentina, 1516-1982. From Spanish Colonization to the Falkland War* (Berkeley: University of California Press, forthcoming), Chapter 7.

3. A generally recognized starting-point for this literature is David E. Apter, *The Politics of Modernization,* (Chicago: University of Chicago Press, 1965).

4. See my description of the *Liga Patriótica Argentina* in *Politics in Argentina, 1890-1930. The rise and fall of Radicalism* (Cambridge: Cambridge University Press 1975), pp. 181-183.

5. Cf. Celso Rodríguez, *Lencinas y Cantoni. El populismo cuyano en tiempos de Yrigoyen* (Buenos Aires: Belgrano, 1979).

6. See Ronald H. Dolkart, "Manuel A. Fresco, Governor of the province of Buenos Aires, 1936-1940: A study of the Argentine Right and its response to economic and social change" (Ph.D. diss., University of California, Los Angeles, 1969).

7. Among the fullest accounts of Argentine politics in 1930-1931 is Alain Rouquié, *Poder militar y sociedad política en la Argentina* (Buenos Aires: Emece, 1983), vol. 1, pp. 181-222.

8. For the FORJA and its relations with Frondizi see Mark Falcoff, "Argentine Nationalism on the Eve of Perón: The Force of Radical Orientation of Young Argentina and its Rivals" (Ph.D. diss., Princeton University, 1970).

9. Corporatism under Onganía is briefly discussed in Alfred Stepan, *The State and Society: Peru in contemporary perspective* (Princeton: Princeton University Press, 1978).

10. Eva Perón, *La razón de mi vida* (Buenos Aires: Peuser, 1951), p. 10.

11. A free translation from *La Epoca*, 26 May 1919.

12. See Ezequiel Gallo Jr. and Silvia Sigal, "La formación de los partidos políticos modernos—La U.C.R. (1891–1916)," in Torcuato S. Di Tella et al., *Argentina. Sociedad de masas* (Buenos Aires: Editorial de la Universidad de Buenos Aires, 1965), pp. 124–176.

13. Quoted in *Hipólito Yrigoyen. Pueblo y gobierno,* ed. Roberto Etchepareborda (Buenos Aires: Raigal, 1951), vol. 1, p. 313.

14. Ibid., pp. 404–405.

15. Quoted in Alberto Ciria, *Perón y el justicialismo* (Buenos Aires: Siglo XXI, 1981), pp. 123–124.

16. Quoted from *El Bimestre Político y Económico* (Buenos Aires: Centro de Estudios de Estado y Sociedad, Jan.-Feb. 1983), p. 96.

17. *La Epoca* (Buenos Aires), 27 June 1918.

18. Quoted in Darío Cantón, "El ejército en 1930: el antes y el después," in Haydee Gorostegui de Torres, *Historia Integral Argentina* (Buenos Aires: Centro Editor de América Latina, 1971), vol. 7, pp. 11.

19. Cf. David Rock, "Machine politics in Buenos Aires and the Argentine Radical Party, 1912–1930," *Journal of Latin American Studies* 1972 (4,2), 233–256.

20. These examples are drawn from press readings during 1972–1983.

21. Cf. Roberto Etchepareborda, *La revolución argentina del noventa* (Buenos Aires: Editorial de la Universidad de Buenos Aires, 1966).

22. Cf. Rock, "Politics in Argentina," Chapter 8.

23. Cf. Rock, *Argentina 1516–1982,* Chapters 6 and 7.

24. Ibid., Chapter 7.

25. Quoted in Stepan, *The State and Society,* pp. 31–32.

26. Rock, *Argentina 1516–1982,* Chapter 1.

27. Ibid., Chapter 2.

28. Cf. Tulio Halperín Donghi, "Revolutionary militarization in Buenos Aires, 1806–15," *Past and Present,* no. 40, July 1968, 84–107.

29. Cf. John Lynch, *Argentine Dictator: Juan Manuel de Rosas, 1829–1854* (Oxford: Oxford University Press, 1981).

30. Quoted in Abel Echegoyen, *La democracia argentina y el partido socialista* (San Fernando: 1946), p. 27.

31. Rock, *Argentina 1516–1982,* Chapter 7.

32. The most complete account of this period is Guido di Tella, *Perón-Perón 1973–1976* (Buenos Aires: Sudamericana, 1983).

2

Can Argentina's Democracy Survive Economic Disaster?

Michael Monteón

It is as if the [financial] centers have gone mad, but we will not pay usury. . . . It would seem as if the developing countries were being attacked with a neutron bomb in reverse, which would leave men, women and other creatures alive, while destroying the nations' productive apparatus. This madness must be ended once and for all.
—President Raúl Alfonsín, May 18, 1984

The revival of civilian democracy in Argentina is the latest response of that nation to a crisis that dates from at least 1930. Since then periods of growth have alternated with those of stagnation and retrogression and only one President has been freely elected and completed his term. As economic frustrations have intensified, administrations and even forms of government have followed one another with dizzying rapidity: the country has had 15 chief executives and 22 finance ministers in the last two decades.[1] Raúl Alfonsín, inaugurated in December 1983, has had to face this uninspiring political legacy and an economy that is chaotic and near a credit collapse. How is he to generate a new set of policies that will simultaneously produce growth and enhance the prospects of democratic government? A few months after he took office, his chances for survival and perhaps even success looked good. Now that he has been President for over a year and half, they look increasingly bleak. He seems to be waiting for some external set of events to rescue the nation from crisis but time is not running in his favor.

I would like to thank Carlos Waisman, David Ringrose and Tom Dublin for their comments on this paper and to thank Graciela Kaminsky for helping me locate some key data.
  Note: This paper was completed in June, 1985.

Argentina entered the twentieth century with bright prospects, offering such high wages that it attracted millions of laborers from southern Europe. It has now become another case study in underdevelopment. Even as late as the 1930s, when it suffered from misrule, it had a rapidly expanding industry. Now it is moving from the status of a semi-industrial to a post-industrial society.[2] The recent experience of most of its manual laborers and its middle class has been of declining real income. This historical "outcome" has befuddled no small number of analysts. The long-term tendencies underlie the contemporary dilemmas and are essential to understanding why Alfonsín's administration is imperiled.

The literature on the country's development is often polemical, but authors of a wide variety of viewpoints agree on two turning points.[3] That of 1930, already mentioned, occurred because of the Great Depression; a democratic order that began with universal manhood suffrage in 1912 ended in a military coup. Thereafter, the political norms of the country became unclear.[4] A civilian government during the 1930s was sustained by agro-export interests (ranchers, wheat farmers, cattle fatteners, and the grain and meat-packing companies), by military force and through fraudulent elections.[5] The next turning point was 1943–46. The military seized power in the name of reform and renewal and one of the officers, Juan Perón, maneuvered within the military regime to build a new political coalition. He succeeded by creating a populist party, the Justicialists, that included military men, industrial protectionists, ambitious bureaucrats, and organized labor. He was elected President in 1946 and then tried to create a one-party state. He lasted until 1955 when another military coup drove him from office. By then he had spent the government into crisis and had severely harmed agrarian exports. Old-line reactionaries in the military, the Church, and the export sectors teamed with offended liberals in other parties to force him out.[6]

These events left the country splintered into paranoid factions. The anti-Peronists, divided into the Radical Party liberals and the reactionaries, distrusted one another because of events in the 1930s when the latter persecuted the former. But the liberals within the Radical Party dared not support a democratization of the country for fear of reopening the door to Perón and Justicialism, with its base in organized labor. One of the central complexities of Argentine politics is the role of the Peronist unions. They are fundamentally undemocratic: when Perón rebuilt the labor movement in the mid-40s, he systematically decimated the Socialists and independent leftists within it. The result was a set of hierarchical organizations, loyal to the leader, run by bosses who were often proto-fascists (or sometimes, plain fascists). Perón and his loyalists had little real interest in the class struggle.[7] But the Peronists have usually pushed for a return to electoral politics and universal suffrage because this is the only setting in which they can hope to gain national office. From 1955 until 1973, military rulers alternated with civilians elected under rules that banned the Justicialist Party. Neither form of government was able to legitimize itself in the eyes of the population.

This political disaster had profound economic consequences because the government had become an essential allocator of the national income. This was not entirely Perón's doing. As David Rock demonstrates in his study of the Radical Party, the Radicals created a mass-based politics of distribution when they first won the presidency in 1916.[8] But Perón extended the trend—a broader political base required more money and meant turning against the exporters, something the Radicals had never done. As early as 1943, the reform junta placed a ceiling on land rents and gave rural workers a minimum wage. When Perón became President, he increased import and export duties, and more importantly, took control of export marketing. The government purchased from producers, was paid abroad in hard currency, and pocketed the spread that accrued as a result of currency devaluations. The consequences of the Peronist policies soon undermined the benefits. Industrialists gained greater protection but then had to pay higher real wages. The middle class gained government jobs; the working class was handed minimum wages, shorter hours and other benefits but then both workers and the middle class lost as wages were eroded by inflation. Yet each sector that had benefitted, however briefly, became afraid of any changes that might generate new losses. Industrialists remained wedded to protection; the middle class, to patronage; the workers, to their corrupt unions. After 1955, those hurt by Perón's policies sought redress. Politics became a zero-sum game; the economy grew a paltry one per cent per year.[9]

The final dilemma for Argentina is a result of its economic dependence on agricultural exports. This is a puzzling development in a country where industry has been the leading sector for five decades. But agricultural exports remain crucial for industry, labor, and the government. Until the 1960s, industry did not export in significant amounts but was dependent on imported capital goods and fuel; when industry did begin to export it could do so only with massive state subsidies. Even after 1960 and until the 1980s, capital goods and fuel made up 40 to 70 per cent of each year's imports while meat and grain made up about half of all exports.[10] Industry is still uncompetitive in the world market, and to sustain it, income has to be transferred from agricultural earnings.[11] In addition, exports directly affect labor because beef and grain are "wage goods," that is consumed by workers. After the 1950s, investment in agriculture fell to the point that the country was unable to export and satisfy domestic demand at low prices. Since the early 70s, governments have used the "veda" or meatless days to promote export earnings. Finally, they have been very reluctant to institute effective taxation. Export and import duties have—depending on the regime—made up 15–28 per cent of revenues.[12]

Export dependence is compounded by the fact that governments have usually run deficits every year since 1955. They have borrowed at home or abroad, printed money and, at times, resorted to a "floating" debt by shorting employees on their checks.[13] During the late 1950s and the 1960s, governments encouraged foreign investment, especially from the United States, in order to accelerate economic performance.[14] The result was that, although imports were usually less than exports, the cost of export profits, patent fees, and debt payments produced an unfavorable balance of payments in ten of the years between 1955 and 1973.[15]

In the late 1960s, the country sank to profound levels of cynicism and despair. The military was once again in power, the economy was faltering, and real wages were falling. Then, in 1969, students at the University of Córdoba joined with workers in that city to overthrow the government. They were put down, but the "Cordobazo" signaled the political arrival of a new generation. The generals began looking for a graceful exit. Catholic students in Córdoba and Buenos Aires, seeking a radical alternative to the status quo, came to believe that Peronism had been a revolutionary vehicle before 1955 and could be one again. A left emerged that included these new student Peronists and others who were Trotskyites. They waged urban, guerrilla war—kidnapping industrialists, robbing banks, and killing a former President—and soon frightened foreign and domestic capitalists.[16]

This was the backdrop for Perón's return. He had been living in Madrid. In June 1973, he came back to Buenos Aires, a "savior" to opposed factions and helped transform the country's long-term problems into its contemporary disaster. The political right counted on the "old man" to put down the guerrillas (although Perón had welcomed guerrilla leaders to his home in Madrid), the left saw him as the leader to revive the popular "revolution" betrayed in 1955, the labor movement and portions of the middle class saw him as someone who would raise their standards of living as he had in the late 1940s. After a series of maneuvers, he was elected President and, in the year before his death, began a rapid replay of his first period in government. Organized labor was courted assiduously and wages rose.[17] The total number of government employees increased from 1.2 to 1.4 million.[18] Taxes on exports were reimposed, tariffs were raised, and industrial output climbed. This populist spending spree quickly led to massive government deficits and higher rates of inflation. Then, just before Perón died, the government shifted policies and demanded sacrifices from labor while courting foreign and domestic capital. Labor lost its gains as wage controls were reimposed (a fate it had often suffered under military and Radical rule).[19] A disappointed guerrilla left revived its war on the state. Isabel Perón, having inherited the Presidency from her husband, used the guerrilla war to unleash the military and Peronist, right-wing death squads against her opponents.[20]

The right, however, saw little reason to keep her in office. The generals took over in late 1976 as the foreign debt reached 10 billion dollars, government deficits amounted to 15 per cent of the gross domestic product, and inflation, for a few months, reached an annual rate of 3,000 per cent.[21] The country's terms of trade—hurt by increased protection for beef in the European Common Market and Perón's tax policies—were only 60 per cent of what they had been in 1970. Most of industry, hit by the soaring cost of credit and imported goods, was contracting. Steel output, for example, fell 24 per cent in a single year.[22] General Jorge Rafael Videla, the first of the military chieftains, took office determined to destroy the guerrillas and reverse the economic collapse. He appointed José A. Martínez de Hoz, scion of one of the great landed families, as Finance Minister. His policies magnified the disaster. They are usually labeled monetarist, which is fair only if the term is given baroque latitude.

Martínez de Hoz did not pursue a straightforward policy in his five years in office. Instead, he oscillated between free-market experiments and extensive intervention, arguing that only a gradual reduction of inflation would avoid massive unemployment. He began by renegotiating the foreign debt with the International Monetary Fund, which, as usual, played the role of broker between creditor institutions and the indebted nation; as part of the deal, the government offered better terms for foreign investment. He sold some state companies. The rate of inflation declined but remained in triple figures. To reduce it further, in 1977, he imposed price controls on 800 companies. For the same reason, the following year, he restricted the flow of capital into the country by imposing controls on foreign bank deposits. These policies left an inflation rate of 140 per cent.[23]

His policies were a repetition of what military governments had tried each time they came into office. Exporters were rewarded, industrialists were protected, labor was repressed.[24] Officially, the government permitted unions but disbanded their national organization, the General Confederation of Workers. In fact, the death squads targeted labor activists. Not surprisingly, wages again trailed price increases.[25]

The Finance Minister often expressed his admiration for the Generation of 1880, his forebears who, working in collusion with British capitalists, created prosperity through agricultural exports and low tariffs.[26] It was not until December, 1978 that any of this seemed more than ideological chatter. Then the second oil crisis and a new surge of petrodollars in international banks that required "recycling" gave him his chance. The first surge, after 1973, helped finance Perón's debacle. But at least interest rates were low. Now, Argentina, like most of the rest of Latin America, borrowed heavily from the almost trillion dollars that banks were anxious to lend, and this time rates rose sharply.[27] Pushed by right-wing ideologues and his own ideals, Martínez de Hoz announced a policy of "convergence," by which he meant that Argentina would opt for a rapid liberalization of economic policies; its economy would meet the terms required to compete freely in the world. This was the "monetarist" period and lasted until he left office in the spring of 1981.

The policy consisted of using imports to systematically force down the price of domestic goods. Tariff reductions accelerated and duties fell from an average of over 80 to only 40 per cent. Devaluations were announced ahead of time and occurred with regularity. All restrictions on capital movements ended.[28] Cheap imports did keep prices from rising as quickly. For a few months in 1980, the inflation rate fell to 50 per cent. Government deficit fell to two per cent of the GDP and exports rose. Martínez de Hoz basked in international acclaim, as hard currency reserves rose from 6.0 to 10.0 billion dollars.[29]

This good news was an illusion. In reality, this was the time of the "bicycle." Private banks, competing for deposits, raised real interest rates to 40 per cent a year. The spread between domestic and foreign interest rates meant that Argentines could borrow dollars abroad, invest them in 30-day accounts, and pocket the difference. The spread also drew in about two billion dollars in "hot" money—foreign investors looking for quick returns. The serious gamblers invested in the stock market where some importing and banking companies, fueled with record quarterly earnings, jumped 1,500 per cent.[30] In a pattern paralleling foreign lending to Argentina, Argentine bankers did not look too closely at the loan recipients. A large number of colonels, whose government posts were their only collateral, borrowed heavily and mounted the bicycle. It was a Ponzi game on a national scale.

Developments in Argentina did converge with those in Chile and Uruguay which were also going through "monetarist" experiments. All three discovered that the immediate damage of low tariffs and unregulated speculation far outweighed any benefits in productivity or in reducing inflation.[31] Structural problems persisted. An open economy gave corporations with access to foreign credit an overwhelming advantage over those borrowing at domestic rates. The latter, already weakened by the

Peronist years, went under rapidly. Balance of trade figures turned sour as an overvalued peso attracted imports while the end of industrial subsidies hurt exports. Many Argentines read the situation correctly and took their money out of the country; they hold an estimated 20 billion dollars abroad today.[32]

The whirl lasted a little more than a year. In April 1980, two private banks, Promosur and the Banco de Intercambio Regional (BIR), failed. The Finance Minister used his influence to spare the banking officers a judicial inquiry.[33] The government had not modified laws that guaranteed bank deposits when it had lifted interest regulations. Covering the liabilities of the BIR, the largest private bank, cost the Central Bank two billion dollars. But this was merely the start. An overvalued peso, expensive credit and falling terms of trade now put even big industry and agriculture on the rack, and the economy plunged. In January, Sasetru, the largest agricultural exporter and an industrial conglomerate, went under with assets of 200 million and debts of over a billion dollars. Fifteen thousand jobs ended.[34] The bank failure spread, closing 72 institutions by March 1981; capital flight cut reserves in half.[35]

Unemployment doubled in six months. Because of the ideological bias that enters many Argentine statistics, no one is certain how bad the situation became. Official numbers admit four to eight per cent unemployment, depending on the region.[36] One study by multinational corporations found 15 per cent of the urban labor force unemployed. Labor spokesmen argue that the reduction in work hours for those employed was the equivalent of another eight per cent.[37] Industrial jobs fell from 1.8 to 1.3 million; many workers became self-employed in the service sector.[38] Defenders of Martínez de Hoz admit that real wages in 1982 were about 50 per cent of what they had been a few years before—labor unions say that wages were only a quarter of what they had been in the one good year of the Peronists.[39] A recent survey concluded that, based on "unmet needs," the percentage of the population living in poverty rose from 7 to 28 per cent between 1970 and 1980— before the bank crash occurred.[40]

As the collapse became evident, General Videla ended his term of office and, as he had promised he would, Martínez de Hoz left with him. General Roberto Viola inherited a situation not unlike that of 1976. His Finance Minister, Lorenzo Sigaut, ended the era of the open economy and reinstituted numerous controls—to little avail. Sigaut found that his only short-term remedy was to borrow heavily abroad, especially to cover the hemorrhaging at the banks. In this, he was able to count on a lag-time between image and reality: international bankers had liked Martínez de Hoz and now considered Argentina credit-worthy.

Viola lasted only nine months—until the image evaporated. General Leopoldo Galtieri took over, decided the country needed a diversion from its economic troubles and, in the spring of 1982, launched the invasion of the Malvinas (Falklands) Islands. The U.K. sent its task force and the diversion ended in military defeat. At the end of 1982, as Galtieri was ushered out of office and Argentina prepared for democratic elections the following year, the country was already behind on its foreign debt payments. Looking at the amounts due, one official of the IMF called it a "financial Hiroshima."[41]

Alfonsín has not been able to correct past mistakes. Since his inauguration (December, 1983), he has begun a multifaceted effort to ride out the situation. At home, this involves building a firmer coalition that includes elements of the Peronist labor movement and the broad spectrum of the middle class. He won labor support during the election by promising a real wage increase of six to eight per cent and by insisting on a democratization of the unions. He has yet to deliver on either promise. Efforts to raise wages have been undercut by inflation and the demands of the IMF vis a vis the foreign debt. The Peronist rank and file is open to new leaders; most believe that their present ones care little about them.[42] But the Peronists dominate the Senate and have frustrated efforts to legislate union reform. In October, Alfonsín forced new elections on about 650 unions (there are about 1,100 in the country) but he pulled back in his attack on the old guard when he saw that younger, more radical candidates were emerging at the shop level.[43] This tactic did not win him labor peace. The young radicals have joined with the older Peronists in demanding wage increases greater than the rate of inflation. Buenos Aires is now under an intermittent siege of strikes.

He has also failed to bring the government's finances under control. The military was running in the red as it left office. With a population of 28 million and a labor force of 10 million, the government employs 1.9 million people. It consumes about the same percentage of the GDP as Scandanavian welfare states but, aside from employment, offers little welfare.[44] The most recent figures list 650,000 employees in national administration, 900,000 in provincial and local administration, 315,000 in state industries and 40,000 in the national bank. This is an increase about a hundred thousand over the end of the military regime. Real wages of most employees were increased as soon as Alfonsín took office, but under IMF pressure, he has had to peg further salary increases to 90 per cent of inflation.[45] The state companies, concentrated in communications, railroads, energy and military goods, are major money losers. So far, the new administration has not found a means to improve their efficiency. It is unwilling to shut them down for fear of higher unemployment. It has cut some expenditures on the military. It has raised taxes and service fees but is spending faster than it is earning. Alfonsín is playing the old Radical game of trying not to offend anyone and of increasing the patronage base—all the while impoverishing the country. Only a few months after taking office, the government admitted it could not meet its deficit target of no more than four per cent of the GDP and settled instead for one of nine per cent.[46] In 1984, inflation rose from 440 to 640 per cent; it is now 800 per cent and climbing.[47]

Argentina's future depends as it always has on trade. As a result of a healthy grain market, it still enjoys a favorable balance of trade. But the massive wheat surpluses in the U.S. may soon cause a sharp fall in grain prices.[48] New oil and gas finds have cut the need for imported fuel, but capital goods are still imported and patent and service fees are still high. The new reality of its political life is that the country cannot pay the foreign debt and improve living standards.

Alfonsín committed a major policy error at the outset of his administration when he failed to insist on a review of all outstanding foreign loans. He could then have raised substantive questions about how much was owed and when, and he could have coupled these questions with others about why a new constitutional regime should have to pay debts acquired under military rule. It would be harder but not impossible to raise such questions now. He has done a great deal to promote a new political morality, one that takes civil rights and democratic procedures seriously. The leaders of the military governments will apparently be tried for mass murder. Instead of imposing a solution to the country's quarrel with Chile over the Beagle Channel, the government held a plebiscite and the populace approved handing over the disputed territory. He has toned down any confrontation with the Thatcher government over the Malvinas and appealed for a negotiated settlement (this has been rebuffed by the U.K.). But if he cannot improve the general welfare of the population because of conditions imposed by foreign bankers, a basic argument for democratic procedures will be lost.

The President knows this. The government has quarreled publicly with the IMF and acquired a reputation among international bankers for contentiousness. In its early months, the administration played with the idea of an alliance among debtor nations—an idea the U.S. press dubbed a "debtors' cartel."[49] But this prospect was undercut by the disparate interests of the debtors, and the fear and respect Latin American political leaders accord the opinion of "advanced" nations. For example, as debtor delegates were meeting at a conference in Cartagena, Colombia, last year, Jaime Lusinchi, Venezuela's new President, announced, "We don't need the discipline of the IMF because we are going to impose it ourselves."[50] Argentine officials also used the back channel of unattributed press comments to hint at a debt default. It was argued that, with its own beef, grain, industry, and energy sources, the country could go it alone.[51] The government tried to increase hard currency reserves and has kept paying suppliers of key imports even when falling behind on debt obligations.[52]

The government and the nation are on a treadmill. The internal credit system is near collapse; the government bailed it out of a bank crash in September 1984 by running the printing press. More recently the central bank has lowered reserve requirements.[53] Yet, the economy is starved for capital, real interest rates soared to 20 per cent a month after the September crisis.[54] With government deficit now at 10 per cent of the GDP and rising, Alfonsín needs all the foreign cash he can get. A major reason the rate of savings is so low is that a four billion dollar trade surplus is pledged to debt payments. (Another, of course, is that no one trusts the banking system.) The economy is also saddled with massive domestic debts; the government is still liquidating companies that went under in 1981–82, owing 64 billion pesos to thousands of creditors. The popular response has complicated official life even further: people buy their groceries on credit cards, using the inflation during the float to cut the bills; an underground economy, centered in services and smuggling, is probably the only "sector" that is growing.[55] The government lurches from one quarter to the next, under the threat of IMF "sanctions" abroad and riots at home. Last September—the month of the banking crisis—the IMF demanded that the government postpone wage increases and eliminate price subsidies on basic goods in order to qualify for new loans to reschedule the debt. The Peronists hit the streets calling Alfonsín a sell-out (and worse) when he agreed.[56] In March 1985, the IMF curtailed any new foreign credits because the government was a billion dollars behind on the rescheduled payments. The trade surplus is not enough to cover these payments; they require at least a two billion dollar cut (out of 4.5 to 5.0 billion dollars) in imports. The government responded by raising taxes on consumer goods; many rates rose 25 per cent.[57] Alfonsín came to the U.S. in March and campaigned for a lowering of tariffs on Argentine exports.

So far, Alfonsín's major asset is that the only alternatives to his government are the Peronists and the military. Each has recently failed in government and is divided and demoralized by the experience. The President can say that the recent past was worse than the present, and he is right. This fact may, as some believe, see him and the democratic process through his term.[58] Perhaps. But Argentine society is in a period of profound introspection, the outcome of which is uncertain.

His popularity may not be enough; future access to foreign capital is jeopardized by decisions abroad. First of all, the country can no longer pretend to meet the technical requirements imposed by the International Monetary Fund; this is openly admitted by its new Finance Minister, Juan Sourrouille. This means non-compliance which means no new foreign loans. Secondly, the U.S. Treasury is already forcing some creditor banks to write down the value of their loans to Argentina. In effect, the Treasury is saying that these loans will probably never be fully paid. Finally, it will take only one of the country's 320 creditor institutions to demand payment and force the issue. Or, a bank that is not heavily exposed in Latin America might, in this period of wildcat competition, decide to buy a small bit of debt, force a default, and use it to wreck the market position of his competitors. This possibility caused one New York banker to openly worry about "some hothead somewhere in the world."[59]

Is there a way out of this mess? Argentina has already taken the first steps toward default by falling behind on payments. The next is an official admission that payments can never be met—a suspension—on all or part of the debt. Default may never occur because both sides have good reasons to avoid it. An official repudiation of the debt legally triggers retaliation; the U.S. Treasury has said it would insist on it. One official asked a business journal, "Have you ever contemplated what would happen to the president of a country if the government couldn't get insulin for its diabetics?"[60] A default would force creditors to write down all their loans to the country at once; several New York banks would face massive capital losses. And, under international agreements, a debtor nation cannot pay some creditors and not others. These legal considerations, however, may have little practical value; bankers will undoubtedly be willing to take what they can get in order to maintain the veneer of partial compliance. Bankers must also consider what might happen if a default did not ruin Argentina, the incentive for other debtor nations to do the same would become overwhelming.

But Argentina is psychologically and bureaucratically unprepared for such a move. The Radical Party has not planned for a default in any public way and has not pursued the internal policies required for a head-on clash with its creditors and their governments. The budget in 1984 was presented by the government months behind schedule. It was out of date as soon as it went into effect. Can a government unable to put its own house in order withstand the calamity of trade retaliation in the event of a debt repudiation?

Debt repudiation need not be an unmitigated disaster. Several Latin American countries recovered in the 1930s when in default of their foreign debts. Any successful strategy for circumventing the debt impasse must center on trade. The U.S. and western Europe take about 30–40 per cent of Argentina's exports and supply half of its imports. A cut-off from these areas would be fatal. The country has been selling about half of its rising wheat output to the Soviet Union; it can expect to keep this market as long as the dollar continues to depress U.S. exports.[61] But the Soviet Union cannot supply Argentina with crucial capital goods, although many of these goods should be available from Japan and other "Pacific Rim" industrializing nations. Most of all, Argentina has to convince the advanced world that having trade without debt payments (or with partial payments) is better than losing both trade and payments. In this respect, Alfonsín is making a mistake to ask for tariff reductions from the creditor countries without publicly pressing the issue of the debt. At home, the government must create a new approach to trade and development that uses the trade surplus to eliminate its deficit and to expand credit for domestic production, that minimizes the use of hard currency to cover imports, and expands the use of barter or "countertrade." Countertrade and counterpurchase arrangments are on the increase and now make up an estimated quarter of world trade. Argentina is increasing its countertrade but its actions have been *ad hoc* rather than coordinated with any larger plan.[62]

With a decent plan to carry it out, a repudiation should work in Argentina's favor. The country, like the rest of Latin America, has increasingly little to lose. A study at the Brookings Institution indicates that even a 20 per cent worsening in the terms of trade as a result of repudiation would cost less than continued compliance with IMF demands. By 1987, according to its calculations, Argentina, Brazil and Venezuela would be on the rebound from repudiation while under current conditions no recovery in living standards is likely before 1990.[63]

The best policy for all concerned would be, of course, to wipe the slate clean. Lord Harold Lever has proposed that creditor nations give their banks 20 years to write down the principal due on these loans while their governments cover the interest. This would cost 35 billion dollars a year at the outset, less as principal declined. By easing the credit squeeze, it would generate an increase in world trade many times more than the debt itself.[64] But this idea is too sensible to be accepted in the world of Ronald Reagan and Margaret Thatcher.

Instead, the crisis worsens despite recent declines in interest rates. When it began in 1982, the world's foreign debt—what each nation owed all others—was a trillion dollars; the Third World owed 700 million. Now, the Third World alone owes a trillion.[65] Interest continues to be compounded and, worse, the U.S. is now a debtor nation and is borrowing more. Sooner or later, the U.S. will have to cut back on its borrowing, reduce the scale of its government deficit and enter another recession, reducing trade income for the Third World and, especially, for Latin America. Optimists see the problem in terms of liquidity—are the countries earning enough to "service" their debts? They argue for better terms of credit for debtor nations and better cooperation on the issue among advanced countries.[66] Such views ignore the history of the debt and the fact that new debts will also have to be repaid—76 per cent of the current debt consists of loans acquired to pay past debts. Henry Kissinger calls for a Marshall Plan for Latin America, ignoring the differences between Latin America and Europe and the many changes in the world economy since 1946.[67] A more relevant parallel is to events in the 1920s and to the unfounded optimism that surrounded the Young and Dawes Plans for financing German reparations and inter-Allied debts. Then as now the debtors cannot pay because of the ways the debt and the world economy are structured. Then as now, creditor nations insist on repayment while raising protective tariffs. The Third World cannot go on as a net exporter of capital; this turns every capitalist generalization about development on its head. Nor can anyone reasonably expect the people of Latin America to accept an indefinite austerity while governments automatically turn over export earnings to foreign bankers.

Within Latin America, the debt plans are already toppling. Brazil, like Argentina, is again in non-compliance with IMF terms. Bolivia suspended regular debt payments in 1984 and declared that it would only pay 25 per cent of its export earnings from now on. Riots in Santo Domingo forced the Dominican government to suspend debt negotiations last year. The newly-elected President of Peru campaigned on a platform that endorsed Bolivia's actions. Ecuador has unilaterally rescheduled its payments. Fidel Castro is rebuilding his status as a regional hero by denouncing the debt burden and urging repudiation. The end of this era is near.

Perhaps the Argentine government does have a plan for the future and is jockeying for the time to implement it. It has initiated some of the elements for surviving debt repudiation. But appearances indicate that it is improvising as it goes along. It has neglected one of the central elements of political survival in a democracy, recruiting public support for a more nationalistic set of policies. Alfonsín is a popular and decent President, unfortunately that is not enough to assure democracy's survival. As I close (June, 1985), the financial quarter is ending and he has just announced an austerity plan that is more sweeping than any before. It includes new taxes, the establishment of a new currency unit and the promise to immediately stop deficit spending. The latter is a "shock treatment" against inflation, a phrase not heard since Pinochet imposed it on Chile in the mid-70s.[68] If the foregoing analysis is correct, then this plan will also fail. Current policies are starving the country of investment, accelerating hyper-inflation, and, by eroding living standards, are leading toward another depression. Argentina's future turns on somehow persuading Alfonsín to forego a future imposed from abroad and fight for the one he promised.

Notes

1. *Business Week,* 6 February 1984, p. 65.
2. Dante Walter Gamba, *La argentina posindustrial: un desafío a la inteligencia* (Buenos Aires: IMPSA, 1981), pp. 184–187.
3. Pedro R. Skupch, "El deterioro y fin de la hegemonía británica sobre la economía argentina, 1917–1947," in *Estudios sobre los orígenes del peronismo,* ed. Miguel Murmis and Juan Carlos Portantiero (Buenos Aires: Siglo XXI, 1973), vol 2, pp. 51–74; Juan Eugenio Corradi, "Argentina," in *Latin America: The Struggle with Dependency and Beyond,* ed. Ronald H. Chilcote and Joel C. Edelstein (New York: Schenkman, 1974), pp. 375–397; and James Petras and Thomas Cook, "Dependency and the Industrial Bourgeoisie: Attitudes of Argentine Executives toward Foreign Economic Investment and U.S. Policy," in *Latin America: From Dependence to Revolution,* ed. James Petras (New York: Wiley, 1973), p. 163; Aldo Ferrer, *The Argentine Economy* trans. Marjory M. Urquidi (Berkeley: University of California Press, 1967), pp. 185–205; Carlos F. Díaz Alejandro, *Essays on the Economic History of the Argentine Republic* (New Haven: Yale University Press, 1970), pp. 254–276; Laura Randall, *An Economic History of Argentina in the Twentieth Century* (New York: Columbia University Press, 1978), pp. 222–237.
4. Alain Rouquié, "Hegemonía militar, estado y dominación social," in *Argentina, hoy,* ed. Alain Rouquié (Mexico City: Siglo XXI, 1982), p. 13.
5. H.S. Ferns, *The Argentine Republic* (New York: Barnes and Noble, 1973), pp. 116–138; Peter H. Smith, *Politics and Beef in Argentina* (New York: Columbia University Press, 1969), pp. 137–169; Antonio Elio Brailovsky, *1880–1982: historia de las crisis argentinas: un sacrificio inútil,* 2nd ed. (Buenos Aires: Editorial de Belgrano, 1982), pp. 95–127.
6. J.A. Paita, "Prólogo," in J.A. Paita, et al., *Argentina, 1930–1960* (Buenos Aires: Sur, 1961), p. 8.
7. Joseph Page, *Perón: A Biography* (New York: Random House, 1983), pp. 66–72, 270–272.
8. David Rock, *Politics in Argentina, 1890–1930: The Rise and Fall of Radicalism* (Cambridge: Cambridge University Press, 1975), pp. 110–114, 272–273.
9. Richard D. Mallon and Juan V. Sourrouille, *Economic Policymaking in a Conflict Society: The Argentine Case* (Cambridge, Mass.: Harvard University Press, 1975), p. 42.
10. Banco de Análisis y Computación, *Relevamiento estadístico de la economía argentina, 1900–1980* (Buenos Aires: Banco de Análisis y Computación, 1982), pp. 222–223, 244–245; James W. Wilkie and Adam Perkal, eds. *Statistical*

Abstract of Latin America 23 (Los Angeles: UCLA Latin American Center Publications, 1984), p. 55.

11. Gamba, *La argentina posindustrial*, p. 184; Carlos Abalo, "Argentina: fundamentos del reordenamiento económico y premisas para una propuesta industrial," Instituto de Estudios Económicos de América Latina; *Argentina: políticas económicas alternativas* (Mexico: CIDE—Centro de Investigación y Docencia Económicas, Septiembre, 1982), pp. 36–37.

12. Fundación de Investigaciones Latinoamericanas [FIEL] *Indicadores de Coyuntura*, Jan. 1979: table 5.1.

13. Banco de Análisis y Computación, *Relevamiento*, pp. 263–264, 283.

14. Jaime Fuchs, *Argentina: actual estructura económico-social* (Buenos Aires: Ediciones estudio, 1981), pp. 22, 272–288.

15. Ibid.; Carlos Abalo, "Argentina: fundamentos del reordenamiento económico y premisas para una propuesta industrial," in Instituto de Estudios Económicos de América Latina, *Argentina*, p. 18.

16. Richard Gillispie, *Soldiers of Perón: Argentina's Montoneros* (Oxford: Oxford University Press, 1982).

17. Guido di Tella, *Argentina under Perón, 1973–1976: The Nation's Experience with a Labour-based Government* (New York: St. Martin's Press, 1983), p. 199; Julio Godio, *El último año de Perón* (Bogotá: Ediciones Tercer Mundo, 1981), pp. 22–30; Gerardo López Alonso, *1930–1980, cincuenta años de historia argentina: una cronología básica*, 2nd ed. (Buenos Aires: Editorial de Belgrano, 1982), pp. 278–290.

18. Gamba, *La argentina posindustrial*, p. 93.

19. *Review of the River Plate*, 173, no. 4210, 20 March 1983.

20. di Tella, *Argentina under Perón*, pp. 72–73.

21. Aldo Ferrer, "La economía argentina bajo una estrategia 'preindustrial,' 1976–1980," in *Argentina, hoy*, p. 114; *Review of the River Plate*, 175, no. 4250, 10 May 1982; Carlos Juan Moneta, "La Política exterior del peronismo: 1973–1976," *Foro Internacional* 20, 2 (Oct.-Dic. 1979), p. 223.

22. Guido di Tella, *Argentina under Perón*, p. 156; Carlos Palacio Deheza, *El plan de Martínez de Hoz y la economía argentina* (Buenos Aires: Ediciones Corregidor, 1981), p. 224.

23. Palacio Deheza, *El plan de Martínez de Hoz*, p. 106; *Latin America Regional Reports: Southern Cone*, 6 March 1984.

24. For comparisons, see Monica Peralta-Ramos, *Acumulación del capital y crisis política en Argentina (1930–1974)* (Mexico City: Siglo XXI, 1978), p. 107.

25. *Latin America Regional Reports: Southern Cone*, 5 March 1982.

26. Palacio Deheza, *El plan de Martínez de Hoz*, p. 340.

27. Charles R. Morris, op-ed page, *Los Angeles Times*, 27 May 1984; William McChesney Martin, et al., "The International Monetary System: Exchange Rates and International Indebtedness," *The Atlantic Community Quarterly* 21, 4 (Spring 1983), p. 37; Karin Lissakers, "Dateline Wall Street: Faustian Finance," *Foreign Policy* 51 (1983), p. 174; Brian Griffiths, "Banking on Crisis," *Policy Review* 25 (1983), p. 22.

28. *Latin America Regional Report: Southern Cone*, 6 March 1981.

29. *Time*, 7 July 1980, p. 59; *Business Week*, 21 July 1980, pp. 78–83.

30. *Business Week*, 2 July 1979, p. 37; *New York Times*, 17 August 1980.

31. Ricardo French-Davis, "Monetarismo y recesión: elementos para una estrategia externa," *Pensamiento iberoamericano*, (1983), p. 175; René Villarreal, "La contrarrevolución monetarista en el centro y la periferia," *El trimestre económico* 50, (1983), pp. 461–471; *Latin America Weekly Report*, 5 February 1982; for a defense of Martínez de Hoz, see Juan Carlos de Pablo, "El enfoque monetarista de la balanza de pagos en la Argentina: análisis del programa del 20 de diciembre de 1978," *El trimestre económico* 50, (1978), pp. 641–669.

32. *Latin America Weekly Report*, 5 February 1982; *Business Week*, 6 February 1984, p. 65.

33. *Latin America Weekly Report*, 4 April 1980.

34. *Latin America Weekly Report*, 9 January 1981.

35. Roque B. Fernández, "La crisis financiera argentina: 1980–1982," *Desarrollo económico* 89 (1983), pp. 84–85.

36. FIEL, *Indicadores de Coyuntura*, February 1982, table 2.1.

37. *Latin America Regional Report: Southern Cone*, 26 June 1981 and 19 November 1981.

38. Martin Andersen, "Dateline Argentina: Hello, Democracy," *Foreign Policy* 55 (1984), pp. 173–177.

39. *Review of the River Plate* 173, 20 March 1983; *Latin America Weekly Report*, 20 August 1982.

40. *Latin America Regional Report: Southern Cone*, 1 February 1985.

41. *Latin America Weekly Report*, 26 November 1982.

42. Ibid., 7 September 1984.

43. *Latin America Regional Report: Southern Cone*, 9 March 1984.

44. *Latin America Weekly Report*, 21 August 1981.

45. *Clarin* (Buenos Aires), Suplemento económico, 5 May 1985.

46. *New York Times*, 14 June 1984; *Los Angeles Times*, 4 July 1984; and Andersen, "Dateline Argentina," pp. 66, 68.

47. *New York Times*, 9 November 1984; *The Review of the River Plate* 176, 9 November 1984; *Los Angeles Times*, 31 March 1985.

48. *Financial Times*, 18 May 1985.

49. *Business Week*, 6 February 1984; *Los Angeles Times*, 12 June 1984.

50. *New York Times*, 18 June 1984.

51. *Review of the River Plate*, 175, 29 February 1984.

52. North American Conference on Latin America (NACLA), "Debt: Latin America Hangs in the Balance," *Report on the Americas* 19, 2 (1985), p. 43.

53. *Washington Post*, 2 March 1985.

54. *New York Times*, 9 November 1984; *Latin America Weekly Report*, 23 November 1984; Gary Hector, "Third World Debt: the Bomb is Defused," *Fortune*, 18 February 1985, p. 50.

55. *Business Week*, 24 December 1984.

56. *New York Times*, 29 December 1984.

57. *Los Angeles Times*, 31 March 1985.

58. Arthur M. Shapiro, "The New Argentina," *New Leader*, 14–28 January 1985, pp. 5–7; 11–25 February 1985, pp. 8–10; 11 March 1985, pp. 10–12.

59. *New York Times*, 12 March 1984.

60. Gary Hector, "Third World Debt: The Bomb is Defused," p. 49.

61. Banco de Análisis y Computación, *Relevamiento*, pp. 267–268; *Latin America Special Report*, December 1985.

62. *Latin America Commodity Report*, 9 March 1984; *Washington Letter on Latin America*, 23 May 1984; *The Economist*, 6 February 1982; and Leo G.B. Welt, *Countertrade: Business Practices for Today's World Market* (New York: American Management Association Briefing, 1982), p. 12.

63. Thomas O. Enders and Richard G. Mattione, "Latin America: The Crisis of Debt and Growth," *Brookings Discussion Papers in International Economics*, 9 (1983), cited in NACLA, "Debt: Latin American Hangs in the Balance," p. 42.

64. Harold Lever, "The Debt Won't be Paid," *New York Review of Books*, 28 June 1984, p. 4.

65. *U.S. News and World Report*, 25 March 1985, p. 47.

66. For examples, see Susan Kaufman Purcell, "Latin American Debt and U.S. Economic Policy," *Orbis* (1983), p. 596; Riordan Roett, "Democracy and Debt in South America: A Continent's Dilemma," *Foreign Affairs* 62, 3 (1984), pp. 718–719; Hector, "Third World Debt: the Bomb is Defused," pp. 46–47.

67. *Los Angeles Times*, Opinion section, 24 June 1985.

68. *Los Angeles Times*, 26 June 1985.

Table 1. Latin American Debts and Debt Service

	Debts in U.S. Billions of Dollars			Debts/ Exports	Debt Service/ Exports
	1980	1984	1985 (March)	1983 (Before IMF Rescheduling)	1983
Latin America	229	340	350	246%	64%
Brazil	64	93	100	359	82
Mexico	52	87	99	275	59
Argentina	27	44	48	424	149
Venezuela	27	34	35	196	32

Sources: Ostry, "The World Economy," pp. 550-551; *Latin American Weekly Report,* 8 June 1984; *New York Times,* 20 June 1984; *Washington Post,* 31 January and 26 March 1985.

3

Toward an Analysis of the Structural Basis of Coercion in Argentina: The Behavior of the Major Fractions of the Bourgeoisie, 1976–1983

Monica Peralta-Ramos

Introduction

Recent decades of Argentine political history have been characterized by the exercise of government through increasingly coercive forms. Little by little, the use of unleashed violence has become the principal method of resolving social conflict. The systematic recurrence to the coup d'etat as a solution to political crisis led to forms of repression unheard of in the history of our country. In the setting of a society shaken by the aftermath of State terrorism, economic crisis and military defeat by a foreign power, in December of 1983—and through an unprecedented electoral victory—the Radical Party seemed to inaugurate a new stage in Argentine political life. A stage characterized by the promise of democratic cohabitation and the search for consensus as the main mechanism of government. Nevertheless, more than a year after that date a series of factors that puts these objectives in check persists. In the following, I will try to isolate one of them and to approach what we could call its structural roots. More concretely, I will try to analyze inflation and the speculative practices associated with it as a result of

This paper sets forth my own interpretation of the conflict among different interest groups in recent Argentine history. In no way does the paper represent the views of the Argentine Embassy.

a particular relation of forces between the main fractions of the bourgeoisie, that is, the most powerful sectors of industrial, financial and
agrarian capital. The systematic confrontation between these sectors for
the redistribution of income, and their recurrence to the exercise of
speculative practices as a form of making their specific demands known,
not only gave rise to the uncontrolled development of inflation. In
addition, it constituted one of the elements that led to the crisis of
institutional legitimacy that has shaken the country in the last two
decades. If this confrontation was evident in periods characterized by
different forms of government (civilian and military), it tended to become
even sharper in circumstances in which a democratic opening made the
possibility of an increase in wage demands the order of the day.[1] The
simple threat of a claim of a greater share of the social product encouraged
the conflict for the appropriation of income. This situation has been
particularly sharp in the period beginning with the call for elections
and the later access of the Radical Party to the government, in December
of 1983.

It would seem that in circumstances in which speculation and un-
checked inflation dominate the political scene, there is an increasing
tendency to believe that the solution to the acute crisis of institutional
legitimacy would reside in the simple use of consensual mechanisms
of government and in the persistence of democratic institutions. Nevertheless, this vision of the present is not only wrong because it is simplistic
but is also condemned to failure. In effect, if the solution to the crisis
of legitimacy that pervades our society were to reside in the simple
operation and persistence of a formally democratic order, this attempt
will be completely distorted by the uncontrolled development of inflation
and speculative practices. These practices not only constitute a mechanism of struggle for the redistribution of income. They also constitute
a powerful corrosion of the most intrinsic values of our system of life,
revealing the relations of power that articulate society. Although it is
not possible to develop this theme within the limits of this paper, it is
nevertheless important to indicate, though very synthetically, some central
theoretical aspects of it.

In capitalist society, the work of individuals becomes part of social
work (or of society) only through the relationships that exchange es-
tablishes directly between products and indirectly—and through these—
between producers. Social relations that connect the work of an individual
with that of another appear as relations between things (goods, money).
Economic relations always appear as relations of exchange between
products of an equivalent value. Thus they are relations of a material
character, impersonal and of an equivalent order. This aspect that the
relationships adopt allows the displacement, the obscuring, of the social

root of exchange. The existence of a particular structure of social relations at the level of production,—a structure that implies an unequal distribution of economic power—disappears behind a setting: the marketplace, where the major actors are objects (money), that circulate according to a legality of their own, on the margin of the will of the producers, even, submitting them to their own laws.

All exchange presupposes a relation of equivalency between the objects exchanged, whatever may be the specific nature of this. Therefore it is basically a relation of substitution, of replacement, or representation. As such, it always introduces a norm and in this way institutionalizes a regulated organization. Consequently any exchange structures relations of power. When this exchange is between products of value in the setting of the marketplace, the market also reproduces relations of power that are established at the level of production between the agents of production themselves. That is to say, it reproduces relations of power that are structured in another setting; that of relations of production.

Now, in a context like the marketplace—marked by material and impersonal relations, dominated by the abstraction of the quantities and proportions in which things are exchanged—individuals act as autonomous and private subjects, independent of each other. In these circumstances, a condition so that they can establish relations of exchange is that facing them society also exists as something material and autonomous, exterior and independent of their essentially contradictory interests. Thus as the ties between their jobs will be represented through a thing—money—it is necessary that the entire social system also take on an impersonal and material form.

It will have to free itself from the agents of production and from its particular interests and adopt the form of a normative structure, of a neutral code, structured around determined principles and values. More specifically, of a code developed around the principles of equivalence of value between objects exchanged, liberty to exchange and equality of opportunities in exchange. And as social relations tend to present themselves in the form of an exchange between products of equal value, the normative structure that rules these relations will tend to become the central nucleus through which a determined conception of the world will be disseminated at the social level and will impregnate all social relations, independently of their content (be this psychological, political, etc.).

The notions of equivalence in the content of the exchanged, and of liberty and equality of opportunities in the exchange will tend to structure the possibility of all social relations in the field of the perception of the different social actors. These values will assume a central importance in the perception that the actors have of their immediate reality. They will constitute the central core of the social contract on which society itself rests.

Nevertheless, there is something else. If the individual is the unit of analysis beginning with which the relations of economic exchange are focussed, these will appear before the perception of the social actors as an inevitable consequence of human necessities, that is to say, as a natural phenomenon, not historical, not temporal. As a consequence, the code that rules these relations will also present itself as something natural and of a universal nature. Both movements will allow the consolidation of the obscuring of the social root of exchange, the fact that exchange structures and reproduces relations of power. In effect, the human necessities that motivate exchange will be perceived as something natural, as a phenomenon of a universal character and not as the product of specific social relations and as a historically determined phenomenon. Likewise, the code that rules these relations will appear as a neutral thing, also a natural phenomenon, an ineludible result of the development of the human spirit and not as a system of norms and values that results from specific relations of power. Society and the present will appear as the best of all possible worlds and not as what they really are: the circumstances within which we live and as such, always capable of being perfected.

These notions of society and of the present, structured around the prevalence of the principles of liberty to exchange, equality of opportunities in exchange and of equivalence of value between the objects exchanged, becomes distorted through the uncontrolled development of speculative practices in the economic area. This occurs because speculation is an activity of an essentially coercive nature, based on the exercise of a certain monopolistic power over resources and information. Therefore, this tends to make it clear that the exchange is not governed precisely by the principles of equivalence, equality and liberty. On the contrary, it shows that the relations of exchange are supported in a situation of asynchrony of power, of unequal development of relations of power, independently of what may be the origin of these relations, or their content. Consequently, speculation creates a context that allows the visualization of exchange as a vehicle of differences, as a mechanism of reproduction of relations of power. In this way, it tends to subvert the code that rules these activities. Therefore it has an essentially explosive character, especially in circumstances in which there is an effort to consolidate a democratic system of government. If this system appears as the most suitable means of legitimizing institutions to the degree that in the same the exercise of government is based on consensual mechanisms, the uncontrolled development of speculation will subvert this intent completely, in making clear the relations of power that structure the social contract on which society is based.

In the following pages, I will analyze the period between the military coup of 1976 and the access of the Radical Party to the government in December of 1983, in light of the evolution of a particular relation of force between the major fractions of the bourgeoisie. I will show that this relation not only explains the uncontrolled development of speculative practices and the resultant inflation, but that it is also one of the factors that determines the chronic political instability of the country in the last decades. Thus the fundamental importance of this phenomenon, not only in understanding the difficulties that the present political situation presents, but also, and most essentially, the future of democratic cohabitation in Argentina.

The Conditions That Structure the Relations of Forces Between the Fractions of the Bourgeoisie

In general terms, the economic growth model followed in Argentina since the beginning of the decade of the 1960s constituted the structural framework of a peculiar evolution in the relations of forces between the most important sectors of the bourgeoisie. In effect, the different governments that followed each other until 1976 shared the same accumulation strategy, based on two great general principles: high tariff protection for industry and stimulation of direct foreign investment in the most capital-intensive branches of industry.[2] This translated into a systematic intervention of the state in the economy with the goal of stimulating the prioritized development of these branches of industry. The state promoted the development of certain industrial sectors through special exchange rates destined to subsidize exports and imports, special lines of subsidized credit for production, high tariff protection and tax exemptions of all kinds. To counterbalance these subsidies to industry, it also established special taxes for agricultural exports, special exchange rates for the same that acted as another disincentive and a systematic control of the internal prices of these products. The combination of these policies brought with it a recurrent transfer of income from the agricultural sector to the industrial. Nevertheless this was not the only effect of this style of growth: it also tended to generate an oversized growth in increasingly sophisticated imports. Diverse factors explain this development, from unregulated trade between parts of the multinational complex and the resulting overbilling of imports, to the incidence at the local level of rapid renovation of technology in the central countries. Under these conditions industrial development did not respond effectively to the tendency toward inequality of the balance of payments that generally corresponds to countries with little industrialization.[3] During this period, the growth in imports was not matched by an equivalent or superior growth in agricultural exports, the country's main source of foreign currency. This style of growth thus remained paradoxical: all expansion of accumulation led by the most capital-intensive branches tended to end in a crisis in the foreign sector, with the resulting impact on the country's foreign indebtedness.

The crisis of the foreign sector and the necessity of finding "easy" foreign currency to face it generated conditions that allowed the agricultural sector to find the economic and political power necessary to press for, and eventually obtain, a circumstantial change in the policies that encumbered it. The paradoxical character of this style of growth contained the conditions necessary for the preservation of the veto power of the most important fraction of the agrarian interests. In this sensc, it can be said that from the point of view of the relations of forces between the industrial and agricultural sectors, this type of development generated a growing conflict between the most powerful segments.[4] The veto power of the agrarian interests made it impossible for the conflict to be settled definitively in favor of industry. Thus appropriate conditions developed for the exercise of growing pressure on the part of both sectors on official decision making. This pressure took different forms. In my opinion, the most important, because of their incidence at the level of institutional stability, were the growing political use of corporate power and the recurrence to speculative practices to provoke sudden transfers of income from one sector to another. The result was the evolution of a very particular situation: the dispute between these two social groups was not settled through a process of negotiation conducive to the conciliation of interests. Instead, it was settled through arbitrary measures, from the government's reactions to the influence of one sector or another's corporate pressure on the state. It was also settled in a more anarchic, diffuse and explosive way, through the development of speculative practices of different types destined to affect the prices of one sector or the other. The result came quickly and inflation was established as a chronic phenomenon in Argentine life. The diffusion of speculative practices was possible due to the monopolistic power exercised by these two interest groups in their respective areas of activities. The high tariff protection and the stimulus given by the state to the development of foreign investment in the most capital-intensive branches of industry brought with it an increasingly monopolistic and oligopolistic control of these markets. This situation, added to the strategic importance of these branches for industry in general, explains that the standards of production and competition that prevailed in them had a decisive importance in the determination of the prices of industry as a whole, and thus in the Argentine economy. Thus, different practices flourished in these branches, destined to exert pressure on prices. Among these, the principal one was accumulation of stocks, shortages, and the consequent black market of industrial inputs and products.[5] Unlike large industry whose prices come directly from its monopolistic or oligopolistic control of the internal market, the agricultural sector has traditionally depended on international prices and state intervention in the determination of its prices. Despite this, when climatic circumstances and the economic cycle permitted, the most powerful segment of the agricultural sector, that related to export business, also resorted to the practice of withholding its products in order to influence prices.

In summary, one could say that the strategy of development applied from the beginning of the 1960s until 1976 was not exactly the product of an agreement between the fractions of the bourgeoisie. Rather, it was the result of the increasingly coercive imposition of the immediate interests of one sector on another. The consequences of this were the endemic growth of inflation, a growing struggle to provoke transfers of income from one sector to another through the pressure exerted by the political activities of their respective corporate organisms, and the spread, more and more openly, of speculative practices of all types. Little by little productive investment tended to be replaced by speculation as the main source of growth of capital.

This style of growth had another consequence of crucial importance for the institutional stability of the country: the development of an increasingly heterogeneous labor market. Although it is impossible for me to develop this theme within the limits of this paper, I believe that it is important to indicate, briefly, a series of phenomena that are associated with this style of growth.[6] To the extent that the branches that led the industrial development in this period were highly intensive in capital, they had little positive effect on the capacity of absorption of the labor force on the part of industry. At the same time, wages tended to depend on the size of the companies and their branch in industry. The practice of paying wages lower than the minimum living wage tended to become generalized in the small and mid-sized businesses and in the branches with the least relative growth. The characteristics that the labor market assumed began to erode the capacity of the labor unions to negotiate wages. The wages actually paid tended to depend more on increases in productivity than on the raises obtained by the unions. As a result, a growing number of unsatisfied demands did not find an appropriate institutional channel for their expression in the unions. Faced by these demands, the different governments that followed one another during this period resorted more and more to the use of coercion: from replacing collective labor agreements with determination of wage increases by official decree to different forms of police repression. Instead of a setting where the reconciliation of interests was possible through efficient union activity and collective labor agreements, a setting characterized by the elimination of the right to strike and increasingly repressive forms of control of social conflict tended to prevail. All this began to shape a progressive crisis of legitimacy for the strategy of accumulation applied, a crisis that took place as much for the major business sectors as for the salaried classes.

The asynchrony between economic power and access to political power through the electoral system has been a trait of Argentine political history. In effect, the social sectors that in different occasions have commanded the greatest quota of economic power have traditionally been incapable of constituting a political party with sufficient electoral support to guarantee them political power through the electoral system. Instead, the route to political power has been through military coups, fraudulent elections and political pressure from these sectors' respective corporate organisms. The same has not happened with the salaried sectors, in the middle class or the working class. Both classes constituted in different historical occasions the vertebral axis of the two main Argentine political parties: Radicalism and Peronism. This circumstance is one of the factors that explains the persistent Argentine political instability. The incapacity of the economic groups that concentrate the greatest power to set themselves up as a political party with sufficient electoral support to compete for access to political power in democratic elections makes clear the eminently restrictive character of economic power in Argentina. They have traditionally been incapable of negotiating, of conciliating interests, of forming alliances with other sectors that make different demands. Arbitrariness and unleashed repression have been used systematically to impose their specific interests and particular visions of the world. At different historical times the salaried sectors have obtained access to political power by democratic means. Nevertheless, as the history of the last fifty years shows, the response was fast in coming and the constitutional governments were overthrown and replaced by military governments.

From the beginning of the decade of the 60s the effects of this asynchronism became more explosive due to the struggle for redistribution of income that shook the whole society, and in particular the most powerful segments of the bourgeoisie. The possibility of a democratic opening, combined with the consequent increase in salary demands that might accompany it, sharpened the struggle between business sectors. Both the speculative conduct and the political pressure exerted through their respective corporate organizations worsened. These circumstances contributed to the erosion of the legitimacy of the political institutions, a legitimacy put into question by diverse factors: from the systematic political banishment of Peronism and the crisis of representation of the political parties accepted by the system to the successive military interventions. Thus an extraordinary situation evolved: the accumulation of economic and political demands did not find proper expression within the existing institutional channels. The result was the progressive crisis of institutional legitimacy that shook the country. Toward the end of the decade of the 60s social protest saw the light of day through different eruptions of violence. Violence was also the main method used to resolve social and political conflict. In this spiral, the repressive activity of the state went on to adopt increasingly "clandestine" forms, forms that violated its own legality. This situation culminated in 1976 with the systematic introduction of what has today come to be known as state terrorism. In the name of God, the Country, the Family and Liberty, concentration camps, assassinations, all types of torture, moral annihilation, and the "disappearance" of people, all proliferated. This was the result of the actions of the repressive forces of the state organized on the margin of its own law. It made clear the profundity of the crisis of values, of the moral crisis that shook important social sectors.

The Military's Economic Project in the Light of the Struggle Between the Fractions of the Bourgeoisie

What was the meaning of the military coup of 1976 with respect to the theme that I am writing about in these pages: the relation between the major fractions of the bourgeoisie and the impact of this relation on institutional stability? In order to try to respond to this question it is necessary to differentiate between the objectives of the official project and the concrete results obtained. As one would expect, these do not necessarily coincide to the extent that the results depend strictly on the capacity of response of the different social actors with regard to the official policy.

Objectives

In my opinion, one of the principal objectives pursued by the economic policy of the military government installed in 1976 consisted of the attainment of a drastic modification of the pre-existing "rules of the economic game," in order to provoke a change in the relations of forces between the major interest groups. In this sense one could say that the government endeavored: 1. To promote a "more harmonic" development between the rural and the industrial sector, taking from industry a quota of the political and economic power previously held and restoring to the agrarian interests part of the privileges lost in earlier periods; 2. To promote the development of private financial capital; 3. To provide incentive for forms of concentration of capital tending to fuse the most powerful elements of the different productive sectors under the predominance of financial capital, thus stimulating the development of economic groups, concentrating economic interests previously dispersed in different economic sectors.

The government initiated the application of its policies with a definition of inflation as a struggle for the redistribution of the income in a way unacceptable to the system.[7] Therefore, the official arrangement revolved around the intent to break up the sectors that in the government's judgment were the main ones responsible for inflation: the working sector and industry. One of the first means adopted was a drastic reduction in wages. The reduction was so large that in the words of the Economy Minister himself, it eliminated wages as a future source of inflation.[8] In this way, toward the end of 1976 real industrial wages were almost 45% below the level of two years earlier.[9] As is publicly known, this economic measure was accompanied by violent repression of the working class, a repression of previously unknown character in the history of our country.[10] The combination of these policies allowed the elimination of wage demands from the political scene. This was a constant during almost the entire tenure of the military government.[11] After this beginning, all the effort of the anti-inflationary struggle centered on the industrial sector. In this sense, the government began by dismantling the complex machinery of subsidies destined for this sector established during decades of industrial development and promoted through the systematic intervention of the state in specific economic areas. In 1976, the government eliminated the special exchange rates and as a consequence annulled the subsidy that the imports and exports of certain branches of industry received. In addition, series of export taxes and special lines of credit destined to promote exports of the most capital intensive branches were eliminated. In a parallel fashion, and in the character of "compensation" to the agricultural sector: export taxes and the special exchange rates for these products that acted as yet another tax were eliminated, and agricultural prices were freed. The effect of these measures was fast in coming: an improvement in the relative prices of the sector was produced (Tables 1 and 2) and an increase in production and exports followed.[12]

With regard to industry, the drastic reduction of wages substantially diminished costs. Nevertheless, this did not translate into lower prices. In effect, far from decreasing, they increased at a staggering rate. Toward the end of 1976 the Economy Minister made certain corporations responsible for exerting pressure on prices through use of "irregular practices," basically the accumulation of stocks and the black market,[13] and he urged the business community to take responsibilities and to accept the new rules of the game. As the situation did not change, toward March of 1977 the government imposed a "price freeze" on the largest corporations for a period of three months. Explaining the reason for these measures the Minister maintained: "We have observed in the past that certain business sectors have taken advantage of their monopolistic or oligopolistic situation in the market to effect frequent or large price increases. I want to warn that we are going to watch these situations very closely and that in that case we will adopt all measures necessary, utilizing the full gamut the State has available, from tariff measures to permit imports, to other types of measures, so that these corporations come to reason and do not use these practices that are illegal in the market. . . . The government is determined to maintain control of the *Proceso*.* To this end, it will not let itself be diverted by nervousness, by impatience, by weak wills or by those who want to change the course for their own benefit or because of sectorial interests."[14] He concluded his speech with a formal demand that the industrial sector "absorb the March wage increase and maintain their price levels of the end of February without transferring in generalized form new price increases of their products during a transitory period that may be approximately 120 days."[15] This was the period of time that the government anticipated would be necessary to reach an agreement with the major industrial corporations on their future price policy. Nevertheless, not all corporations accepted this agreement and, as will be seen, the effects of the policies subsequently adopted were very disparate.

Toward the end of the freeze it became apparent that large sectors of industry resisted abandoning their traditional methods of affecting prices. As a result, the government, faced with the new inflationary stampede, kept its promise, and not only announced the implementation of a tariff reform aimed at ending the privilege of high state protection but also implemented measures of "another order": the financial reform of June 1977 and by the end of 1978 the "*tablita*," or schedule planned increments in exchange rates, lower than the rate of inflation.

The financial reform of 1977 consisted of a decentralization of bank deposits, the freeing of interest rates, and a law of financial institutions. One of the objectives pursued by the financial policy was to put an end to subsidized credit and thus to obstruct the possibility of accu-

---

Proceso was the name chosen by governmental leaders to denominate this period.

mulation of stocks, shortages and the black market of specific industrial inputs and products. As will be seen, these measures did not have the desired effect, so in November of 1978 the government imposed the tariff reform completely. The terms originally established to reduce tariffs of different industrial products were harmed, damaged by the government itself in its eagerness to chastise the sectors and corporations that did not accept the changes in the rules of the game and realized with anticipation their expectations of future inflation.

In December of the same year the government introduced what would be its most formidable tool to control industrial prices: the *"tablita."* It is estimated that toward the end of 1980, and as a result of this policy, the true value of the *peso* in relation to the dollar was 40% higher than that of 1977.

In the beginning both the tariff reform and the exchange policy pursued the objective of flooding the internal market with cheaper industrial products in order to obligate local industry to lower its prices. Nevertheless, the objectives pursued were not limited to combating inflation or to swaying the industry's capacity to determine internal prices. Like the financial reform, these measures tried from the beginning to impose a drastic restructuring of economic activity. If with the reform the government tried to stimulate a violent transfer of income to the financial sector in order to promote the constitution of economic groups dominated by financial capital, with the tariff and exchange policies it tried to instigate a greater concentration of industrial capital and the imposition of a new model of industrial development based on the leadership of certain branches of industry: agroindustries. The veto capacity of certain business sectors made some of these middle and long-term objectives progressively lose force in the official proposal. In effect, it could be said that faced with the negative reaction of certain sectors of industry to the official proposal, and consequently with the persistence of inflation, the government remained more and more enclosed in the contradictions of a changing policy that not only tended to dismantle industry's capacity to determine prices but that also quickly exercised a negative influence on productive activities in general. In spite of this, some of the objectives proposed were fully realized.

Effects of the Economic Policy

As a consequence of the financial reform of June of 1977, the growth of real interest rates in the internal market was so considerable that in the period of José A. Martínez de Hoz they exceeded the growth of the real interest rates effective in the international financial market (Table 3). At the same time, the local spread was one of the highest found in the international financial market. These two phenomenon were aided by a massive influx of foreign capital,[16] a transference of resources from the productive sectors to the financial sector, and the development of all types of speculative practices in the local financial market. The official guarantee on total deposits,[17] the limited amount of capital required to open a bank or a financial institution,[18] the lack of supervision or control of financial activities on the part of the Central Bank, and the enormous profits obtained—beginning with the existing relation between an always negative interest rate for deposits and a strongly positive interest rate for loans—(Table 4) all explain the overexpansion of the financial system (Table 5). Between 1976 and the end of 1979 the number of branch banks grew at a cumulative annual rate of more than 28%, that of main banks grew at a cumulative annual rate of 23.1% and that of financial institutions 27%. This growth in the number of financial institutions was paralleled by a high degree of concentration of capital in the financial market. In effect, toward the end of 1982, 13% of the total number of commercial banks controlled 68% of the total net worth and 65% of the total of the loans.

The result was a situation distinguished by the enormous gains realized by the different fractions of the financial sector. On the one hand, a small core of large commercial banks captured the benefits derived from the existing economies of scale in the banking sector and also windfall profits that arose from the great spreads necessary for the survival of the smallest and most inefficient financial institutions. The latter remained in the market thanks to the official guarantee on total deposits, the negative interest rates for deposits and positive interest rates for loans and the practice of passing on the enormous spreads to the savers and borrowers. The inexistence of control or supervision on the part of the Central Bank made it possible for different speculative practices (or "*bicicletas*") to flourish in the financial market. While this situation allowed all financial sectors to realize enormous profits, from the beginning there was a strong segmentation of the financial market, which was divided between the banks and institutions with access to local and international financial markets, and the banks and institutions that only had access to the local one. The first group specialized in low-risk clients: the large corporations with foreign ties. The second group, on the other hand, depended exclusively on the financial resources obtained locally, and, in order to compete with the first group, it offered greater interest rates and specialized in high risk corporations with little or no access to foreign credit. Access to foreign credit, cheaper than that obtained locally, in a financial market with the characteristics described above, made it possible for a reduced number of institutions to realize enormous profits.

The policies applied had multiple and uneven consequences on the industrial sector. From a global perspective, the recession initiated in the mid-70s was accentuated: the participation of industry in the gross national product changed from 33% in 1976 to 28% in 1983. Toward the end of 1982 the total value added of the industrial sector was less than in 1970 and the labor force employed in industry had been reduced to 73% of the level in 1970. On the other hand, the policies applied accentuated even more the fragmentation of the industrial sector that existed before 1976.[19] In effect, they introduced a new divisive axis: to remain under tariff protection or not. One group,[20] which included the majority of the branches that led industrial development in the period before 1976, stayed highly protected. This group registered important increases in production, in productivity, in the profits/sales coefficient and in investments between 1976 and 1980. It also had easy access to foreign credit. The other group, increasingly submitted to the competition of imported products, had little or no access to foreign capital and registered decreases in production, in the coefficient profits/sales and in investments. It also registered a growth in productivity similar to that of the first group. In both groups there was a drastic reduction of the labor force employed.[21] The corporations that pertained to the second group adopted different tactics to survive, depending on their size and their degree of access to foreign credit. A general recourse was the strengthening of property ties with the financial sector. For many corporations that previously lacked these ties, they became a guarantee of survival during this period. Another recourse was to become an importer and supplier of services of the products previously produced. Many companies reduced their activity to a minimum hoping for a policy change, while others chose to merge. Of course, the small and mid-sized companies were the main victims and many were literally erased from the scene.

With regard to the agricultural sector, after the first year of extremely prosperous prices derived from the measures initially taken by the government, the sector—and again especially the small and mid-sized corporations in the less productive areas—was increasingly damaged by the rise in the price of credit that resulted from the financial reform, and by the exchange policy adopted at the end of 1978. During the period 1976–1980—and with the exception of what happened in 1977—international prices of agricultural products tended to be considerably above domestic prices (Tables 6 and 7). The freeing of agricultural prices, promised by Martínez de Hoz, did not succeed in satisfying the traditional hope of the sector: the balancing of domestic prices with international prices. Apart from this, whole sectors found themselves damaged by climate factors and by the lowering of international prices of some key products. The combination of all these factors severely damaged the small and mid-sized companies that lacked property ties in the financial sector and had no access to foreign credit.

It is important to consider the anti-inflationary policy of the government and its effects on the relation of prices between sectors. As was said above, the improvements granted to the agricultural sector between 1976 and 1977 were translated into a notable improvement of the prices of their products in relation to the prices of industrial products. However, this situation did not last. Between 1978 and 1979 the growth of the prices of domestic industrial products exceeded by 10% the growth of prices of agricultural products. Toward 1980, this margin of difference was 20%. Apart from this, the industrial sector itself did not register a homogeneous position with regard to the evolution of its prices. In effect, the prices of products produced by the sector that remained protected varied substantially in relation to the evolution of the prices of the sector that was increasingly submitted to the competition of imported products. Until 1979 the two groups increased their prices in a similar proportion. From then on, their respective price policies tended to diverge. The group submitted to the competition of imported products registered a growth of 60% in their prices between 1979 and 1980. The group that remained protected increased them about 90%.

Throughout the period of 1976–1982 the prices of domestic industrial products grew more rapidly than the prices of imported industrial products. Further, toward 1980 domestic industrial prices, relative both to the prices of the agricultural products and to the prices of imported industrial products, were higher than in 1970. This is also more significant if one takes into account that in 1970 the official policy was characterized by high tariff protection for industry in general and by numerous price controls. It is worth noting that the policies applied by Martínez de Hoz's team had not managed, in the latter part of their passage through the government, to revert the capacity of certain sectors of industry to determine prices in a monopolistic or oligopolistic fashion. Nor could they prevent the spread of the effects of these production guidelines and rivalry, necessarily affecting the industrial sector as a whole. Perhaps this can be explained by the high interpenetration of property between the large industrial, commercial and financial corporations that existed in the period before 1976,[22] and the characteristics assumed by the local financial market after the reform of June of 1977.

In effect, one of the results of the subsidized credit policy that prevailed beginning in the sixties was precisely the establishment of strong ties between the large corporations located in the officially promoted leading branches of industry and the private financial sector. The principal beneficiaries of the subsidized interest rates were the large corporations tied to the institutions that gave credit.[23] This situation conditioned the capacity of response of the most concentrated sector of industry before the anti-inflationary policy of the government. Apart from this, the easy access to foreign credit on the part of this sector allowed it to adapt readily to the financial reform changes introduced in June of 1977, and to realize enormous profits in the local financial market. At the same time, the characteristics assumed by the latter stimulated the development of new ties between industrial and financial business fractions. The result was the meteoric development of new economic groups, some of which rapidly came to establish themselves as the main national banks. In this way the local financial market transformed itself into a privileged setting for the struggle for the transfer of income between business sectors. This struggle adopted the form of a struggle between economic groups, differentiated among themselves by their possible access to the international financial market and by the type of industrial corporations that constituted them: high or low risk according to the branch in which they found themselves, and consequently according to the degree of tariff protection that they could still sustain. As a consequence, the financial market became the main scene of speculative activity, an activity that led the whole system to the edge of disaster in 1980.

Another consequence of the policies applied in this period was the enormous growth of the debt (public as well as private) in *pesos* and in dollars. High domestic interest rates and the low rate of nominal devaluation stimulated the rapid flow of foreign capital. To the degree in which foreign credit was cheaper than that which could be obtained in the local market, the common practice of institutions with access to the international financial market was precisely to obtain credit abroad and recycle it in the local financial market. In this way, productive investments were replaced by short-term investments in the financial circuit. Between 1979 and 1982 the total foreign debt grew at a cumulative annual rate of 36.7%. The short-term public debt (with a term of less than one year) grew in the same period to an annual rate of 62.1%, the private grew at 43% annually. State companies were used as magnets to attract the flow of foreign capital necessary to equilibrate the balance of payments and to support the exchange policy of the government. From 1978 until the beginning of 1981 these companies were encouraged to contract foreign debt even when the social pressure to obtain a devaluation became stronger and stronger, and the overvaluation of the *peso* became more and more evident. As a result of this management of state companies, their foreign indebtedness grew from 3.1 billion dollars at the end of 1977 to 9.2 billion in March of 1981.

Pressure of the Business Sectors

One of the first measures adopted by the military government in 1976 consisted of a rigid control of the activity of the political parties, the labor unions and the business entities. Businesses, and in particular those tied to industry, were submitted to a process of restructuring controlled by the government.[24] From the beginning the government counted on the explicit support of the group of business organizations that formed the core of the agricultural and financial sector and the reticence and, in certain cases, the opposition of the corporate organisms of industry. Nevertheless this situation did not last long, since the heat of the measures adopted by the government produced a split within the agricultural and industrial sectors. The adhesion in one case, and the opposition in the other, were no longer unanimous.

The process of restructuring to which the business entities were submitted and the rigid control of political activities led to a disintegration of the political pressure exercised by the business organizations. This did not mean, however, the disarticulation of the business community's capacity for opposition to the government. On the contrary, this constituted the axis of the pressure exercised on the government—a pressure that adopted the dangerous form of speculation and an inflationary stampede, with its consequent impact on the stability of the government itself and the legitimacy of the Armed Forces. If in March of 1977—as seen above—the Economy Minister believed it was necessary to publicly urge the main corporations to leave aside their monopolistic and oligopolistic practices in the determination of prices, to believe in the *Proceso* and in the capacity of the government to lead, to believe in the official impossibility of changing the course of this policy, when faced with sectorial pressure—toward the end of 1979—he exhorted them "to believe once and for all in the continuity of the program that is being carried out. I want to tell you today to remember that this program is not the program of President Jorge R. Videla or the program of Minister Martínez de Hoz, it is the program approved by the Armed Forces and as such will continue in its application and in its great general outline after March of 1981. So do not continue thinking that the change is going to take place in March of 1981, because you are going to be wrong again."[25] A few days later he would reiterate the same in a speech at the Stock Exchange, adding "those who don't believe this will run the risk of drowning themselves in their own current. It is time for the blind to begin to see, and the deaf to listen . . . be sure that there will not be another opportunity, and there is no other than consolidation of the *Proceso*."[26]

What had happened? The "Statute of the Revolution" of 1976 anticipated a change in the presidency of the Military Junta in 1981. This circumstance made possible an acceleration of the struggle for hegemony between the different military branches[27] and within the Army itself. This translated itself into a struggle between factions to impose their respective candidates to the Presidency in 1981. The heat of the political temperature on the rise, the business organizations found from 1979 on the opportunity to exercise political pressure on the different factions of the armed forces in order to obtain a change in the policies that hurt them, and in particular a change in the exchange policy. The government thus became progressively more isolated, finding open support only in the most highly concentrated sectors with access to the international financial market. The combination of the political pressures exercised on the different Presidential candidates and the stampede of speculative activity that began to shift toward the foreign exchange market in the face of the possibility of a devaluation created a climate of great political instability. The crisis of confidence of the business sectors was translated into a strong outflow of foreign capital. These financial flows had their consequent impact on the balance of payments and the official exchange policy. The doubts about the continuity of the official economic policy provoked a rise in "irregular practices" of all types.

The government's response came quickly: on one hand, it provided a strong stimulus for state companies to take foreign credit. This influx of foreign currency allowed it to counteract the outflow of capital and the pressure exercised by the black market on the official exchange rate. On the other hand, it also intervened in the main national financial institution—the head of an economic group of meteoric development— the *Banco de Intercambio Regional* (BIR). The moment elected for that and the reasons alleged[28] made it clear that the government was inclined to do anything to maintain the official policy. Soon intervention in three other national financial institutions, also located among those with the largest local capital, followed. Between April 1980 and March 1981 the government intervened in or liquidated 62 financial institutions that together controlled 20% of the deposits. That is to say, it used all its force to settle the struggle between economic groups. Nevertheless, it did not limit itself to the elimination of the most intractable, of those who were most opposed to its policies, but it also interceded to save certain financial groups threatened by the general uncertainty. The consequence of the intervention of the BIR was the appearance of hordes of savers that withdrew funds from the institutions considered most vulnerable and turned them over to foreign and official banks. Many of these funds were diverted toward the purchase of foreign exchange in the black market. In the face of the possibility of bank failure, this market came to occupy a privileged place in the development of speculative activities. In this way, the crisis of confidence tended to become general and the possibility of a bankruptcy of the financial system was the order of the day. The government then intervened in order to save certain financial institutions threatened by the crisis, granting them special lines of credit. Between 1979 and 1980 these lines grew 50.2%, between 1980 and 1981 they grew 81.9%. From 1980 on, the demand of the fractions of the bourgeoisie was precisely the liquidation of the private debt through the granting of special lines of subsidized credit. This was also the principal axis of the dispute among corporations, and of speculative activity.

In summary, toward the end Martínez de Hoz's project had obtained partially successful results. The measures adopted produced a violent transfer of income toward the financial sector and encouraged enormously the concentration of capital and the establishment of economic groups based on the merging of business groups located in different economic sectors. The struggle for appropriation of income between the principal fractions of the agricultural and industrial sectors passed to a second plane, and what predominated in the political and economic scene was precisely the struggle for the transfer of income between different economic groups. These were differentiated on the basis of two main axes: their degree of access to the international financial market and the degree of risk at which their capital was exposed. As a result of this struggle, the financial market was transformed into a privileged place for the development of speculative activities. The government did not manage to impose on industry a consensus with respect to the new rules of the economic game and the capacity of certain sectors to determine prices remained intact. As a consequence of the persistence of inflation, the government continued enclosed in a tactic that was more and more taking away from it the business support which it had counted on from the beginning. In a political arena progressively heated by the struggle between factions of the Armed Forces to impose their own candidates for Presidency of the Junta, and in the context of uncontrolled development of speculative activity in the financial market, the dissident economic groups found an optimal occasion to apply political pressure for a change of economic policy. The immoderate response of the government to this pressure provoked a threat of general bank failure, and with this threat the political instability of the military government became the order of the day.

The Collapse of the *Proceso* and the
Speculative Activity of the Economic Groups

In March of 1981 the transfer of the Presidency foreseen in the "Statute of the Revolution" of 1976 finally took place and General Roberto Viola assumed the government. His reign was shortlived, and it was plagued with contradictions. Faced with the capital flight, the new administration opted for a systematic devaluation, thus putting a final end to Martínez de Hoz's exchange policy. But it went even a little further, and to the surprise of the deposed economic team it restored the duality of exchange markets prevalent before 1976, increased the duties on agricultural exports and designated a special commission constituted by members of the Ministries of the Treasury and Finances, Agriculture and Industry, in order to evaluate the effects of the tariff reform, and to make recommendations for the immediate and medium-range future. That is to say, it seemed that the new government was taking a forced step backward, and returning to the model of development prevalent in the country in the period before the coup of 1976. Nevertheless, the circumstances were now very different.

From the beginning it was clear that the new administration inaugurated a period of acceleration of the tensions between sectors. The confrontation between agriculture and industry to gain priority for their specific sectorial demands reemerged. To this will be added the confrontation between economic groups in the financial market. As another symptom of these tensions, the Ministry of the Economy was divided into five ministries, each one corresponding to a specific clientele. The different business sectors exerted pressure to reestablish lost privileges, or to maintain those recently acquired. However, the main pressure on the government was to liquidate the private debt. Responding to this, the government announced in June a plan to refinance 50% of the debt of the industrial sector and 40% of the debt of the agricultural sector. The struggle between these two sectors to obtain a better quota of the refinancing delayed the application of the plan and limited its achievements. Also in June the Central Bank introduced a system of official guarantee of exchange rates to cover the foreign loans of the private sector with maturity dates that had been extended at least 540 days beyond the original dates of payment. The initial premium paid by the Central Bank under this plan was only 2% monthly and although the rate was raised later, it always remained below the devaluation rates that prevailed at the time. The stimulus was great for the private sector to maximize its use, to the point of creating a fictitious debt. In effect it is estimated that some 5 billion of the foreign debt originated in an exit of capital by this means alone. In this way, the type of subsidized credit given by the Central Bank so that certain fractions of the bourgeoisie could pay their foreign debt was used precisely for these ends. It generally left the country in the concept of "paper-loans," or fictitious debt created abroad by residents of Argentina with the sole goal of qualifying for this type of subsidized exchange.

The capital flight aggravated the situation of the reserves. This led the Central Bank to offer swaps in foreign money to the private sector in December of 1981, applying a monthly premium of 5%. These operations were then suspended but were later resumed, in June of 1982, as part of the scheme to liquidate the delays in payment of the private foreign debt. In September 1982, the swaps represented 5.6 billion dollars. Toward the end of the same year they represented 7 billion dollars. In turn, the contracts with a guaranteed exchange rate grew from one billion dollars in June 1981 to 11 billion dollars in September 1982. Although later they tended to decline, toward the middle of 1983 they still represented some 7 billion dollars. To assess the losses that these different types of subsidies to the private sector represented for the Central Bank is a difficult task. However, a conservative estimate is that they represented 1% of the Argentine gross national product in 1981, 3% in 1982, and 5% in 1983. In any case, these measures had an immediate effect on the indebtedness of the private sector, and in particular of the industrial sector.

In 1980 the short-term foreign debt represented 65% of the total foreign debt of this sector. Toward 1981 this had been reduced to 33% of the total. However, this did not silence the protests, and the pressure exerted on the government to obtain a total liquidation of the foreign debt. Thus these measures were reestablished in 1982 and again in 1983. The subsidies given according to this concept explained a good part of the growth of the foreign debt. In effect, it is estimated that of the total of some 35 billion dollars of the foreign debt contracted between 1976 and 1982, 54.2% corresponded to capital flights, with a large part of this in the concept of self-loans or "paper loans," eligible for the benefits derived from the different programs of subsidized exchange rates (swaps, forward contracts with guaranteed exchange rates) offered by the Central Bank.[29]

It is also important to consider the fortune of the private debt contracted in *pesos*. As was said above, the government of Viola tried to find a solution for this through a bond issue, but this did not manage to satisfy any of the interested parties: the financial institutions and the industrial and agricultural companies. The solution would have to come one year later, with another military government.

In effect, the tensions accumulated during the period of Viola culminated with an internal coup, and a new general—Leopoldo Galtieri—assumed the Presidency in December of 1981. The first measures adopted presaged the return of the policy applied by Martínez de Hoz's team. However, its possibilities of continuation deteriorated as a result of the Malvinas-Falkland War, the fall of the government and the total crisis of legitimacy of the Armed Forces. In a totally new political situation, another general—Reynaldo Bignone—assumed the Presidency. Faced with the evidence of the failure of the *Proceso*, of the shattering of the principal supports: the Armed Forces, of military defeat by a foreign power, and of the possibility of an acceleration of the social tensions accumulated over time,[30] the new government promised to hold elections within a year. This simply intensified the fractions' protests about the liquidation of the private debt. The new government's response consisted of the financial reform of Domingo Cavallo.[31] The results were drastic. It is calculated that as a consequence of the financial measures adopted in June of 1982 in only 6 months 40% of the debt of the private sector was liquidated. The proportion of uncollectable loans in relation to the total net worth of the commercial banks was also reduced quickly. If in December of 1981 they represented 60.6%, in December of 1982 this figure was only 10.2%. The obligations of the private financial sector were partially liquidated through strongly negative interest rates. In only one month these arrived at the minimal level of −18%. The reaction of the different sectors of the bourgeoisie before this liquidation of the debt was not precisely an increase in productive investments. If the government's financial reform aimed at provoking a transfer of capital from the financial sector to the productive sectors, what it really managed was an increase in the speculative activity in the exchange market and a growing capital flight.

In summary, the liquidation of a good part of the private debt under Cavallo's scheme of financial reform, and the subsidies given by the Central Bank in the concept of contracts with guaranteed exchange rates and swaps, not only influenced in a decisive way the foreign indebtedness of the public sector and the massive fiscal deficit. They also gave a greater stimulus to speculative practices of all types, and in particular in the exchange market. The dissociative behavior of the different segments of the bourgeoisie also translated into an even greater fall in the fixed investment and an increase of tax evasion of all types. In 1983 the proportion of taxes collected to the total expenses of the public sector was 46%.

With the passing of the months and faced with the evidence that the promised elections were inevitable, the inflationary phenomena also accelerated notably, and together with it new speculative practices flourished. To the speculation in the financial sector, in the black market of industrial inputs and products, in foreign exchange, was now added the so-called "informal" market of money between large corporations. This financial black market corrodes the financial system in its entirety today and hinders enormously the control of the same on the part of the Central Bank.

So the government elected in October of 1983 arrived to power in the fourth year of an economic recession, in the middle of an inflationary stampede of more than 600% annually, a deficit in the public sector equivalent in the fourth quarter of 1983 to more than 20% of the gross national product, real wages that fluctuated around the levels reached in the 1970s, unemployment and underemployment around 10% of the economically active population, the reserves of the Central Bank in a calamitous state, a heavy foreign debt a third of which had payments due in 1984, and with access to the international financial markets severely restricted. But this was not its worst inheritance. From this perspective, one of the greatest obstacles to the consolidation of democracy in the time period initiated with the access of the Radical Party to the government is precisely the dissociative conduct of the main fractions of the bourgeoisie. Before the official promise to stop the deterioration of the living standard suffered by the popular sectors throughout the different governments of the *Proceso*, the struggle for the transfer of income between interest groups was stimulated even more. If at the beginning of the 1980s this activity put in check the stability of an apparently irreducible military government, today it threatens the possibility of a democratic coexistence. Speculation, with its aftermaths of corruption and violent transfers of income not only threatens the stability of institutions, it also corrodes the values of democracy itself.

Notes

Translated by Carolyn A. Morrissey.

1. The theme of the crisis of Argentine institutional legitimacy has been developed in Monica Peralta-Ramos', *Acumulación del capital y crisis politica en la Argentina (1930–1974)* (Mexico: Siglo XXI, 1978), pp. 170–325. Passim.

2. An analysis of the strategy of accumulation applied from the beginning of the decade of the 1960s and a comparison with that applied between 1946 and 1955 can be found in Monica Peralta-Ramos', *Etapas de accumulación y alianzas de clase en la Argentina, 1930–1970* (Buenos Aires: Siglo XXI, 1972). This book is also included in Monica Peralta-Ramos, *Acumulación del Capital,* 1978, pp. 56–150.

3. This situation arose from the deterioration of the exchange terms of primary goods, which constitute the main export products of these countries.

4. For these we understand: the most concentrated sector of industrial capital, and especially that located in the strategic branches of industry, that is to say in the most capital-intensive branches; and the agricultural sector tied with the export business.

5. The overinvoicing of imports was also a powerful recourse utilized on specific occasions, and in particular in the decade of the 1970s.

6. An analysis of the alternatives assumed by the labor market in Argentina and its relation with the evolution of workers' demands and institutional stability has been developed in Monica Peralta-Ramos, *Acumulación del Capital*, 1978, pp. 102–170, 373–441.

7. In the words of the Head of the Advisory Cabinet of the Ministry of Economy: "Inflation is the expression of the social struggle with regard to income. All that agitates this struggle carries with it inflationary potential. In some aspects, the economic policy applied from April 2, 1976 carries this danger since it aspires to introduce profound changes in the economic life that will be carried out through modifications in relative prices (the financial reform and a more open economy are the most relevant changes) that can in turn introduce responses in the interests affected, which manifest themselves through the price system" *La Nación*, (Buenos Aires) April 3, 1979.

8. *La Nación* (Buenos Aires), 2 June 1976.

9. If there is no indication to the contrary, all the statistical material utilized in this paper is from the World Bank, *Economic Memorandum on Argentina* (Washington, D.C.: World Bank, 1983); ibid., 1984; and from World Bank, *Argentina, Special Report: Private sector impact of the 1976–1980 economic program* (Washington, D.C.: World Bank, 1982).

10. According to the report presented by the Comisión Nacional Para la Desaparición de Personas, CONADEP, to President Alfonsín in September 1984, of the 8,960 people who disappeared that were registered therein: 30.2% were workers, 21% students, 17.9% employees, 10.7% professionals, 5.7% teachers, 5% others, 3.8% housewives, 2.5% military personnel, 1.6% journalists, 1.3% actors and artists, and 0.3% nuns and priests. Comisión Nacional Sobre la Desaparición de Personas, *Nunca Mas* (Buenos Aires: Eudeba, 1984) p. 480.

11. Space limitations have not allowed me to analyze the situation of the working class during the period studied. It is generally maintained that this social sector is the main one responsible for inflation in Argentina. Nevertheless this period is particularly interesting because it shows just the opposite. It is difficult to remember a more savage period in our history with regard to the control of social protest. Despite having practically liquidated any protest, having literally erased it from the political scene, the government could not control inflation. The social pressure accumulated during years only threatened to come to light again toward the beginning of 1982, stimulated by the evident crisis of the *Proceso* and the growing political instability. This explains the invasion of the Malvinas-Falkland, and the later call for elections. But this happened in the framework of the growing deterioration of the *Proceso*, basically the product of the struggles between fractions of the bourgeoisie.

12. Agricultural exports grew at a cumulative annual rate of 16.3% between 1976 and 1980.

13. *La Nación* (Buenos Aires), 20 December 1976.

14. Ibid., 9 March 1977.

15. Ibid.

16. It is impossible to go deeply into an analysis of the international situation that made this phenomenon possible. Nevertheless, it is good to remember that

if certain characteristics that led to an enormous mobility of financial flow had not existed, the result of the economic policies applied in Argentina would have been very different.

17. It is good to remember that this was imposed on Martínez de Hoz's original project by the Comisión de Asesoramiento Legislativo (CAL), and in particular by the influence of the Navy and the Air Force.

18. For example: in Chile—since December 1983—the minimum capital necessary to operate a bank is 8.2 million dollars and that for a financial institution is 4.1 million dollars. If this criteria were applied in Argentina, of the 203 private banks registered in 1983 only some 60 would remain standing, and of the 102 financial institutions existing at the same time only 4 would remain authorized to operate. In addition, of the 60 banks that would remain, 17 would be official, 25 would be private with national capital and 18 would be private with foreign capital.

19. In the period prior to 1976 industry fragmented through different criteria. On one side there was one group, with dynamic growth, essentially composed of the branches that produced intermediate goods, durable and capital goods. In these branches the large companies tied in one form or another with foreign capital predominated. On the other hand, there was a group composed of the branches that produced salary goods. In these the small and mid-sized companies with national capital predominated. These branches had a vegetative growth during the period. Monica Peralta-Ramos, *Acumulación del Capital*, 1978, pp. 102–150, 325–373.

20. The group that remained highly protected consisted of the following branches: petroleum and derivatives, plastics, cement and other non-metallic minerals, transport material, pharmaceutical and chemical products, printing houses and publishers, cigarettes and tobacco. The group that was submitted to the growing competition of imported products was in turn composed of: food and beverages, textiles and clothing, leather and footwear, paper and cardboard, glass and porcelain, iron and steel, metal products, equipment and certain chemical products.

21. Between 1977 and 1980 the protected group registered cumulative annual growth rates of product, productivity and employment, on the order of 1.90%, 3.71% and –1.76% respectively. The other group registered the following annual growth rates of product, productivity and employment: –0.9%, 3.72% and –4.47% respectively. The greatest restriction of occupied manpower took place precisely in the group submitted to foreign competition.

22. World Bank Economic Memorandum on Argentina, (1984) p. 210.

23. Ibid., p. 231.

24. One of the first official measures was the dissolution of the *Confederacion General Economica* (CGE), a business entity that had had a prominent performance in the period prior to 1976. In 1973, the *Unión Industrial Argentina* (UIA), which was the nucleus of the most concentrated sector of industry, was joined with its former adversary, the CGE, and shared responsibility for the economic policy applied between 1973 and 1976. In 1976, after dissolving the CGE, the military government reestablished the former UIA as the only exponent

of the industrial sector and submitted it to a strict process of internal restructuring controlled by an intervener. In 1979, the new authorities that arose from this process of reorganization were institutionalized.

25. *La Nación* (Buenos Aires), 28 November 1979.

26. Ibid., 6 December 1979.

27. Unlike what happened with other military coups, that of 1976 was characterized by the lack of a clear hegemony of the Army over the other armed forces. From the beginning, this was disputed by the other two forces (and particularly by the Navy), as was clearly evidenced by their division of different public institutions among themselves. On the other hand, a clear hegemony of the governing faction did not exist within the Army either. This became clear in the arduous negotiation to select a common candidate for the Presidency of the Junta.

28. It is good to remember that the BIR's intervention took place at a time when the political dispute for the presidency of the Junta between Admiral Eduardo Massera and the group led by General Videla was growing more violent, and the time period established by the Statute to name a President of the Junta had run out. According to newspaper accounts at the time, there was a close relationship between the economic group controlled by the BIR and Massera's group. It is also good to remember that the Central Bank had known about the financial situation of the BIR for a while, since it had named an official with a rank equivalent to that of an intervener, to be in charge of that institution. Thus it could have intervened earlier, but did not.

29. 37% of this debt corresponded to the service of the country's foreign debt itself, 28.5% to unregistered imports—basically of arms and military equipment—and 7.4% was due specifically to the growth of the reserves. World Bank, (1984) p. 17.

30. The invasion of the Malvinas-Falkland Islands was immediately preceded by a period of high tension characterized by the call for a worker mobilization to demand increases in wages.

31. President of the Central Bank, June 1982.

Table 1. Price Increases in the Different Production Sectors: Percentual Changes in Relation to the Former Period. 1974-1977.

	1974	1975	1976	1977
Wholesale Price Index	20.0	192.5	499.0	149.4
Agricultural Price Index	10.0	144.9	526.6	163.6
Non-agricultural Domestic Price Index	23.9	208.6	469.2	146.9
Non-agricultural Imported Price Index	36.9	257.5	690.4	126.2

Source: World Bank, *Economic Memorandum on Argentina* (Washington, D.C.: World Bank 1983); ibid. 1984 and World Bank *Argentina Special Report: Private Sector Impact of the 1976-1980 Economic Program* (Washington, D.C.: World Bank 1982).

Table 2. Price Increases of the Different Production Sectors: Percentual Changes in Relation to the Former Period. 1977-1983.

	Cost of Living	Wholesale Prices			
		Gral Index	Agricul-tural	Non-Agri-cultural Domestic	Non-Agri-cultural Imported
1977	176.0	149.4	163.6	144.4	126.2
1978	175.5	146.0	141.6	147.6	75.9
1979	159.5	149.3	150.7	148.7	93.0
1980	100.9	75.4	63.0	80.1	74.5
1981	104.5	109.6	93.8	112.2	157.7
1982	164.8	256.2	293.5	234.8	377.1
1983	343.8	360.9	373.5	358.8	335.7

Source: World Bank, ibid.

Table 3. Real Interest Rates Prevalent in the Local and International Financial Market. Annual Average in Percent. 1976-1980.

	Local Rate	International Rate
1976	-60.0	-54.8
1977	20.0	- 5.3
1978	21.4	-22.0
1979	6.9	-18.4
1980	29.9	- 9.5

Source: World Bank, ibid.

Table 4.   Real Annual Interest Rates for Deposits and Loans. 1976-1983.

	Deposits	Loans
1976	-65.14	-65.04
1977	-19.78	- 0.66
1978	-14.61	11.92
1979	- 9.43	2.48
1980	- 4.38	25.91
1981	9.51	7.03
1982	-15.13	-12.42
1983	- 9.56	-18.44

Source: World Bank, ibid.

Table 5.   Evolution of the Number of Financial Institutions.   Rates of Cumulative Annual Increase.   1977-1979 and 1979-1983.

	1977-79	1979-83
Commercial Banks (1)	23.4%	-0.77%
.-branches	8.1	3.1
National Commercial Banks (1)	35.26	-2.75
.-branches	17.0	3.36
Foreign Commercial Banks (1)	5.56	9.85
.-branches	2.57	9.36
Financial Institutions (1)	27.0	-7.2
.-branches	52.2	0.29

Source: World Bank, ibid.

(1) References to main branches.

Table 6.   Grain Price Index, Argentina and USA. 1970:100.

	Argentina	USA
1976	87	122
1977	120	101
1978	98	110
1979	78	104
1980	68	119

Source: World Bank, ibid.

Table 7.   Meat Price Index, Argentina and USA. 1975-1980.

	USA	Argentina
	Export Prices	Domestic Prices
Average 1975-1977	109	99
First six months 1979	126	100
Last six months 1979	150	118
First six months 1980	136	99
Last six months 1980	138	91

Source: World Bank, ibid.

Table 8.   Evolution of the Price Index of Different Industrial Groups. 1977-1980.

	1977-78	1978-79	1979-80
Protected Group	162.1	137.3	98.1
"Competitive" group	156.0	146.3	56.0
Domestic Non-agricultural Wholesale Price Index	156.5	130.6	60.7
Imported Non-agricultural Wholesale Price Index	75.9	93.0	61.7
Consumer Price Index	175.5	158.4	84.0

Source: World Bank, ibid.

Table 9.   Index of the Average Real Wages of the Public Sector (1950:100). 1970-1983, selected years.

1970	127.3
1972	118.8
1974	180.4
1976	96.2
1978	98.0
1980	123.5
1981	120.7
1982	92.1
1983	101.0

Source: World Bank, ibid.

4

Changes in Argentine Society: The Heritage of the Dictatorship

Juan M. Villarreal

1. It is customary to analyze social change from the standpoint of economic trends. But society, production, and patterns of consciousness are fraught with power. Changes in the social structure, in the simple customs of daily life, in the categories of prestige that traverse the communal fabric, as well as the contradictory process of the formation of social classes that follow the path of fragmentation, are marked by the imprint of power through subtle and changing, yet manifest, patterns. Production, society, and power are not autonomous fields that respect each other's fixed, static and univocal relationships. Rather, they are interrelated aspects of the social fabric, permanently subordinated to the dynamics of historical time, that modifies them, alters their relationships, and frequently changes their relative determinative weight, or promotes the conjunctural role played by some of them.

In treating the changes that have occurred in Argentine society, particularly with regard to its occupational and social structure, I will emphasize the perspective of power. The productive conditioning of an historic relationship of dependency, recently more severe, will be present in my discussion, but the core of my analysis of the social change left as its heritage by the dictatorship will be an overview, from the perspective of power. I will deal with those changes in the social structure as effects of power. I do not imply that other possible explanations—such as the one which takes the economy as a point of departure, for example— are invalid, nor will I even try to assert that the power perspective contains greater deterministic strength. I will simply try to recover a view of society from the elusive terrain of politics, at a certain historical conjuncture, and presupposing a certain explanatory power, from this perspective, for the changes that have occurred recently in Argentine society.

2. What is power? What is implied in the analysis of the political, social and economic effects of the dictatorial government under which Argentina lived so tragically in recent years? Would such an analysis be an attempt to identify the protagonists of the state administration, to analyze the body of laws established, and to detect the interests involved? Power is something much more diffuse, general and complex than a form of government, its protagonists or its laws. It is constituted by a variable network of relations of force that runs through the whole of society, producing diverse effects, by a complex weaving of relations of domination not truly recognizable in the simple opposition between those governing and those being governed, and it is not situated only at the level of the administration of state power. Hence, such a perspective is not that of a struggle among sectors, classes or parties, striving for a power that is external to them and one which they can seize. It is, rather, the coexistence of multiple relationships of power at distinguishable points and levels, running like a complex network through the institutions, parties, social groups, state apparatuses and ideological tendencies.[1] Here one can see the interweaving of diverse strategies, the fragmentation of power and the permanent movements of accumulation or loss of power, with its continuing variability.

From this perspective, the military government established in 1976 is more the product of circumstances than an agent implementing a preconceived plan. This government was the outcome of a general process of a regressive reply to the advances in radicalization, struggle and conscience developed by the popular sectors in the years just prior to its accession to power. This process implied a considerable concentration of power while, at the same time, it was a repressive application of power at points, instances and in diverse groups, in an unprecedented manner in Argentine history. In its entirety, this regime was an attempt to carry out a general restructuration of the relations of power existing in the social formation. It was not so much, then, as a regressive social process, just the implementation of an "open" economic policy, or the regressive redistribution of income—all of which was also done, but the substantial modification of the relations of power, their bases of support and the organizational forms that expressed them, in order to restore a social order that had arrived at a crisis.

3. This work will not analyze in detail, then, the general conditions of the political-military process, nor even its economic repercussions, but fundamentally the changes in the social structure it produced, seen as changes in the bases of the relations of power.

In Argentine history, the industrialists and the agrarians, an economically-dominant conservative elite without mass support, as well as the mass parties (the nationalists and liberals, Peronists and Radicals, civil and military factions), have expressed, with their peculiarities—which imply the formation of relationships of force manifested at different points and levels, with their own inflections and specific transitory nature, the constancy of mutually exclusive politico-ideological confrontations. These cleavages prevented the formation of a strategy of a lasting hegemonic domination in order to ensure socially acceptable rules of power.

The permanent crisis of production, society and power in Argentina, with successive alternating forms of domination, with social explosions that revealed the ungovernability of the society, with contradictory politico-economic projects that substituted each other, was due to a variety of reasons. Here I will concentrate on one aspect of the problem, without professing to exhaust or invalidate other partial explanations. This aspect is the peculiar configuration of a social structure heterogeneous at the top and homogeneous at the bottom.

The multiple recurrences of discord between agrarians and industrialists, landholders and capitalists, speculators and producers, and large and small owners with their aftermaths of permanent conflict in the last 50 years of Argentine history reveal a heterogeneity of political interests and political orientations in the ruling groups, and the impossibility of establishing a relatively stable project of domination. On the other hand, at the bottom, the early capitalist industrialization, the high level of urbanization, and the generalized weight of wage relationships—in conjunction with other determinations which it is pointless to analyze in detail here—resulted in a peculiar degree of relative homogeneity among the subordinate classes on the basis of common localization, generalization of wage labor, and similar work conditions. Relative homogeneity, I say, compared with the greater part of the situations throughout Latin America, but which did not prevent, in any event, the diverse lines of cleavage already experienced by the subordinate classes, as I will point out later on.

Tables 1 and 2[2] illustrate these traits. The peculiar Argentine combination of a high weight of employers and also of wage earners in the active population expresses the coexistence of diverse strata of owners, as well as the great diffusion of wage labor. As regards the distribution of occupational sectors, the comparatively high proportion of nonagrarian laborers indicates the preponderance of urban workers. In Argentina—even though the past decades show a slow process of "Latin-Americanization" of the social structure—we see, against the comparative background of Latin America (with its peculiar combination of centralization and independence), a situation characterized by a high proportion of middle-level owners who bring about heterogeneity in the ruling sectors, and an appreciable development of wage relationships which homogenize the subordinate classes. Let me add at this point that wage workers altogether represented 72% of the active population in 1960, while workers connected with material production formed 52% of the total number of wage laborers. This clarifies the meaning of the term social homogeneity, which I used above. Most Latin American countries (Chile and Uruguay are exceptions) show an inverse situation of homogeneity at the top and heterogeneity at the bottom, i.e. different structural conditions. Some central countries that I have indicated— Great Britain in Table 1 and the United States and Great Britain in Table 3—present, schematically-speaking, and at first glance, homogeneity at both levels of the social structure. That same peculiarity in the Argentine society, differentiated from capitalist centers and the rest of Latin America, is still seen in the information shown in Table 3, referring to 1970, even though it is attenuated by the aforementioned process of Latin-Americanization.

4. Now, the process of formation of Peronism occurred on the basis of utilizing the conjunction of interests that made possible a society that is relatively heterogeneous at its peak and homogeneous at its base, but the movement persisted over a period of forty years, developing power effects that were to fortify its bases of social support. Populist power permanently reproduced the bases of its own power, in a molecular and subtle form. Industrialists against agriculturists, the modern bourgeoisie against the traditional one,[3] middle-level owners against monopoly capital: all, due to their relative weakness, sought out the support of the working masses. They fostered an industrial development channeled toward the domestic market that required an appreciable redistribution of income, giving a general tone to populist policies and making possible a harmonization of interests with the workers. These encouraged the industrialist, statist, nationalist and redistributive nature of the movement, but they frequently threatened to go beyond in their demands, and to come into conflict in the factory with their political allies. Workers frequently threatened with the specter of a labor power grown beyond acceptable limits. Socially homogeneous and in ample majority, the wage laborers (and among them, the industrial workers), strengthened their capacity of resistance to power by their Peronist political unity. This unity implied a contradictory popular and national conscience, but in the struggle it frequently surpassed the limits of that manifest conscience and expressed more advanced latent forms.

Strengthened, beyond their relative ideological-political subordination, by the heterogeneity and contradictions of the dominant groups, the Peronist workers—serving as a nucleus to other popular sectors, began to present themselves, at the beginning of the seventies, as a virtual threat to the established order, as a probable third alternative in the conflicts between industrialists and agrarians, nationalists and liberals, civilians and the military. It was the threat of a corporative project which, more than resting on the conditions of objective feasibility, rose on the political scene owing to the fluctuations in the ruling class, the crisis of ungovernability, and the hegemonic stalemate. But it also arose due to the weakness, diffuseness, and contradictions of the propertied group that shared the populist project with workers and middle-class sectors.

This process coincided in time with the development of various guerrilla movements channeled toward a radical change in the system, but mainly with one of them that was linked to the Peronist youth, and which gained considerable weight in Peronism as a whole. With a strong neighborhood influence, and a considerable presence of middle sectors and some labor support, these groups carried out practices that questioned the legal monopoly of force. They were the protagonists of a new phenomenon of power in Argentina that altered the traditional framework of the relations of force and appeared, in the face of hegemonic disputes and the disarray of the status quo, as a threat to install a different social order.

It is not that the radical Peronist youths led the mass of workers, nor that the workers sought to radically change the established order. It was, rather, a dangerous combination: the homogeneous mass of wage earners (with its mobilized working class nucleus) with its growing social power and economic weight, was strengthened by the political power conferred on it by its unity with the Peronist party and by the active presence of radicalized youth sectors. The latter fostered more profound changes and were stimulated by default, by the inability of the dominant groups, linked with populism, to evolve a stabilizing, developmental plan that would articulate the diversity of interests embodied in their political identity. Social chaos and the power vacuum, despite the rightist trend of Isabel's Peronism, failed to guarantee the maintenance of order.

5. Under these conditions, a military takeover occurred in March of 1976. The problems faced by the new regime were fundamentally political in nature and perhaps, in one of the clearest cases in recent Argentine history, its economic, social, and cultural policies were subordinated to the aims of a regressive power strategy prompted by the dominant social forces. It was not so much a coherent strategic elaboration planned by the power holders, as the effects of power resulting from a reactive social process: it was a response to the economic, cultural, organizational, and political advances that the popular sectors had experienced in the previous years in all areas of social life.

The greater toughness of the employers with their wage workers in regard to their working conditions, the overt or self-imposed cultural restrictions, as well as the terrible repression brought to bear on popular organizations—among other points and at levels at which a devastating authoritarian, but multiform, power was established—express the multiplicity of systematic power exercises without a subject that confronted fundamentally three social actors: Peronism, the workers, and the guerrillas.

It could be said that the military lowered real wages abruptly to combat inflation; that they de-industrialized the nation in order to increase the efficiency of capitalist production, by opening the domestic market to foreign competition; that they liberalized the capital market in order to stimulate the efficient use of financial resources; that they eliminated the restrictions on entry of foreign capital in order to promote economic development; or that they proclaimed the subsidiary nature of the state with its aftermath of privatization in order to control the fiscal deficit and to stimulate the rapid growth of private capital. These were the manifest aims of the economic program, which seemed to have considerable autonomy as regards the power represented by the military, to such a degree that the political seemed to be subordinated to the economic, Videla to Martínez de Hoz. These objectives seemed to be geared toward the fostering of economic development, greater efficiency of the economy, and the maximization in the use of available resources. From this perspective, we can say today that the economic plans led to a complete failure.

But were these the truly fundamental aims? Is it valid to affirm that politics was subordinated to the economy? I believe the contrary to be true. From the perspective of a strategy of power, those economic aims, as well as their apparent failure, take on a new light under which their failure becomes relative.

The latent aims of the economic program, subordinated to political needs, were a part of an ensemble of complex power effects, because the regressive social process expressed by the military administration was complex. Without exhausting all their implications, these objectives were to confront, to destroy, to beat on, and to divide its enemies. Peronists, workers and guerrillas, the three main privileged actors of the preceding Spring, were attacked, in their life, liberty, income, working conditions, their capacity for political action, and the social foundations of their power bases. If the foundations of the social power of the popular sectors rested on—among other factors which I will not go into deeply here—that peculiar structural combination in Argentine society of heterogeneity above and homogeneity below, with the consequent economic, cultural and fundamentally political implications; if that was the problem, then a series of measures had to be implemented to restructure society by inverting the terms of the equation.

This does not mean that the search for homogeneity in the dominant sectors linked with the heterogeneity at popular levels would be the work of an omniscient subject, that it might result from the deliberate application of a political plan based on effective laws, or that it might arise from economic-political steps taken by a brilliant team of intellectuals at the service of the dictatorship. Power strategies resulting from a regressive, complex, multiform social process, such as the one developed in Argentina in 1976–1983, frequently go beyond the conscience of the protagonists and produce changes that are hard to detect on the basis of their relationship with the legislation promulgated or with the aims explicitly formulated. They are molecular changes in the social structure that are developed quietly, without causing a stir, but which restore its image to power by changing the relations of force, and by creating new conditions for the political game. They are similar, perhaps, to the deep currents of the sea that take time to surface and which result in a complex configuration of waves.

It would be naive to deny here the role of economic determination. Simple economicism is not consistently surmounted by inverting the terms of the causal relationship, in an absolute manner which causes one to think that everything that occurs in society is the result of an omnimodous power. It would be a mistake to deny that changes in the social structure were the effects of economic development, secular problems arising from the stagnation of Argentine economy, and the peculiarities of subordinate reproduction.

6. Nevertheless, just as there were economic determinants that induced the centralization of capital, more significant were the policies that were implemented to accelerate this process, in the framework of the regressive social process that brought about a high concentration of power in the hands of a military elite, finance capital, landowners, and monopoly capital. The best conditions in history were present for its realization.

The attempt to homogenize society from above began by bringing into play an ample gamut of resources in conjunctural circumstances that had created conditions favorable to the unification of sectoral interests. The populist disorder, worker's defiance, and the threat of subversion had caused the defenders of order to tremble. Their central interests had been threatened and there was no room for minutiae, trifling niceties or the defense of special interests. The centralizing mechanism, accelerated by the power holders, created conflicts, but political conditions did not allow secondary frictions to be placed on the agenda at the same time as changes could be made in the structural conditions of heterogeneity of interests at the top. These changes might bring about the dreamed-of return to the calm times of oligarchic domination.

The verified concentration of economic power produced a satellization of small capital, foreign competition instigated by tariff policies brought about the bankruptcy of a multitude of middle and small entrepreneurs, and economic problems pushed some producers into commercial or speculative activities. Some small entrepreneurs undoubtedly fell into the informal sector.

The figures in Table 4 illustrate both the decrease of employers in the active population, which expresses the disappearance of small property owners, and the growth of the self-employed which expresses, in part, the fall of entrepreneurial groups in the informal sector. In this way, by centralizing economic power, by destroying or weakening small entrepreneurs, a homogenization of dominant sectors around a productive, financial and commercial elite was achieved. The bourgeois bases of the populist project were thus diminished.

But there is a second important aspect in this process of social homogenization and articulation of interests. It is the problem of hegemony. The presence of bases for social conflict among sectors, levels or groups at the summit of dominance rested on the double phenomenon of social heterogeneity and hegemonic disarticulation. To homogenize dominant interests and to promote a hegemonic sector or group that would articulate, through negotiation, the multiple sectoral demands, are the two parts of the same power process consisting in the unification of domination. The regressive process we are studying attempted to establish the predominance of finance capital. This sector, capable of connecting the various sectoral interests, appeared as the most suitable to exercise hegemony and, due to its special ability to centralize capital, it became the most appropriate one to oversee the process of homogenization from above of the dominant sectors.

In this way, homogeneity and hegemony would make it possible for the ruling class to confront the subordinate sectors with multiplied power. Moreover, the world crisis and its more acute repercussions on the Argentine economy had brought to the fore that form of capital that is abstract, mobile, and favorable to speculation. This type of capital would have more to gain from the unforeseeable mechanisms of high inflation, with its erratic sectoral fluctuations. The "opening outward," the liberalization of the capital market, and increased financial dependence were other factors that gave greater power to the financial sectors. These factors were linked with the great expansion of private international banking.[4]

A third general aspect of the process of homogenization from above, attempted as a power strategy and the most evident as a political resource, was the military leaders' plan to convert themselves into a military party that would integrate the multiplicity of interests of the dominant sectors.

The problem of social heterogeneity of a class, or of an aggregate of social sectors with hegemonic inclinations, is compounded when combined with political disarticulation, or, more categorically, when manifested by a lack of political expression. This lack seems to be evident in the productive, financial and commercial elites of Argentina, from the time of the 1930 crisis onwards. The old Conservative Party that unified them remained in the remote past. The articulation of sectoral interests, and the presentation of elite interests as general interests in order to permit the incorporation of sectors from the masses and the ideological integration of parties, are problems which have not yet been resolved by the great bourgeoisie of Argentina. Under these conditions, economic domination does not correspond to political domination, and the country continues along a complex path of political instability, crisis and ungovernability.

When these conditions worsened, and corporative proposals appeared which revealed the ascendancy of the workers and potential threats to subvert the status quo were made, the military defenders of public order and an elite jealous of its prerogatives found a common field of action: power. Unified in the face of guerrilla action, worried over mass mobilization, and pushed to the control of the state by the ineffectiveness of the last phase of the Peronist government, the military assumed the defense of the status quo. But to guarantee public order meant to defend the interests of the dominant classes, security, ideological purity, efficiency and productivity. In this way, perhaps the most ephemeral because the military in the government once again felt the crosscurrents of the sectoral interests of civilian society, they tried to operate, beyond their individual consciences, as a military party that would close the circle of homogenization, hegemony and representation of the interests of Argentina's dominant sectors.

7. The attempt—the result of a not completely conscious power strategy without a subject to guide it, but rather the resultant motley mosaic of social, political and economic measures—to heterogenize the popular sectors was much more complicated, with origins that went further back in time. It was connected, too, and thus it can be confused in power terms with, structural determinations that arise from the situation of dependency. But isn't dependency also a project of power, a relation of forces from within and without our societies?

If one attempts to analyze the character of the popular sectors from the viewpoint of power, bearing in mind the bundle of relationships of force which constitute this power, and considering the different levels at which power is manifested, it is advisable to be more precise. Let us differentiate among social, economic and political power.

In referring to the social power of certain groups (whether socio-economic classes, primary groups, political parties, institutional groups or ideological tendencies, and considering that I am referring basically to social groups as classes) I will make reference to a series of aspects: their quantitative weight itself, their degree of social homogeneity given by similar living or working conditions, the social projection of their prestige as an evaluated group, and the level of differentiated self-awareness or ideological cohesion that empowers them to act in common. It is difficult to establish, *a priori*, without an exhaustive empirical study, the weight that each of these traits has in the equation of social power, but it does appear clear that power is the result of a combination of them.

The economic power of the social groups also results from the conjunction of various dimensions: the groups' relative participation in the social product, the technological development of the activity in which they participate, the level of income they receive, and a last and essential point, the degree to which they are located on a nuclear point in the chain of economic activity. Greater precision should be given to this last point: with the development of monopoly capital, the growing socialization of the processes of work and the greater integration-diversification of productive activities, the economic linkages that articulate the diverse activities in terms of input-output, of raw materials, productive equipment, labor force, means of consumption, money capital, and commercial capital and services, develop more and more. In these economic linkages, certain activities become an economic nucleus of integrated complexes of economic activity (for example, in some Latin American countries, the terminal phase of the auto industry), and certain integrated complexes become an economic nucleus of the whole set of productive activities in the society (for instance, the industrial complexes of production of durable goods, also in some semi-industrialized Latin American countries). The bonds of certain workers to these economic nuclei promotes both their relative economic power as well as their ability to bargain at the union level. The combination of these afore-mentioned factors determines the economic power of the social groups. Obviously, this applies directly when we refer to social classes, fractions or strata, but it also has indirect application to other groupings, such as parties or movements, in which case the problem would consist in determining the labor or economic insertion of its members.

With respect to the political power of the social groups, that is, their capacity to play an active role in specifically political relations of force, it is determined by traits like the following: their degree of political cohesion expressed in recurring practices, the organizational level, the tradition of struggle, and the direct or indirect control of sources of institutionalized political power. In the last instance, this is where power relations are concentrated, where social contradictions are resolved, and where the fundamental changes in the power relations among social classes, political parties and ideological tendencies take place.

8. I will start by analyzing the case of the industrial workers, the classic sector where the popular masses agglutinate. This group became, during the years of proscription (1955–1973), the linking axis of Peronist resistance.

I mentioned that relative participation in the social product is a constitutive element of the economic power of social groups. The policy of lifting tariff barriers, of making the economy more efficient and of transferring industrial resources to other sectors, which was carried out by the military and other regressive forces from the state apparatus and other instances of power, produced a dismantling of industrial production, a wave of company bankruptcies, and a considerable absolute and relative reduction in the aggregate value of manufacturing. Table 5 illustrates this process clearly: the industrial sector declined from 29% of the gross national product in 1975 to 25% in 1980.

One may speak of an effective policy of de-industrialization, caused by the need to strengthen the agricultural and livestock sectors, by the advisability of introducing a higher level of efficiency in the whole of the economy, or by the interest among the financial capitalists to channel productive capital toward circulation associated with centralization of capital. But the combination of all these factors fails to explain the unusual and a-historical process of deterioration of industrial production. More precisely, these factors contribute to the clarification of the phenomenon, but the dimension of power must be added in order to complete the explanation. And consistent with my hypothesis, which subordinates production to power among the objectives of the "process of reorganization," de-industrialization became a fundamental aspect of the power strategy put into play, because it subtracted economic and social power from the two fundamental actors: the middle-level industrial property owners and the manufacturing workers, who were the axis of the alliance between industrialists and laborers, the social nucleus of populism, of that political movement that had sheltered "subversives" with a level of mass support that had not been seen in Argentine history for the last half century.

Some workers, many of them, would continue working in industry, but for shorter hours. By attempting to avoid laying off workers so as to prevent the generation of explosive situations, and by reducing the average hourly wage, the employers thus decreased still further the workers' income by reducing the number of hours worked. Table 6 illustrates this point, showing the drop in man-hours worked in industry. The index was 100 in 1970, 119 in 1974, 104 in 1978 and 84 in 1981. It shows clearly that this phenomenon was especially accentuated in the textile, clothing, shoe, and machinery industries. The latter—the production of electric and non-electric machinery—shows a considerable reduction in the hours worked, thus revealing the symptomatic decline of a fundamental sector for the supply of equipment to the rest of industry and for the stimulation of the reproductive process in general.

A similar thing happened to wages, the purchasing power of which declined alarmingly in percentages variously calculated at between 40 and 60 percent during the period from 1974 to 1982. The real wages of Argentine workers fell—in 1976 dollars—from 217 in 1974 to 109 in 1978, which shows the considerable decrease in the standard of living and the market power of the workers; purchasing power, but also the power to finance their organizations, and economic capacity to exercise class solidarity.[5]

Not only the workers' economic weight was reduced through a restrictive wage policy, but also they were divided by means of wage stratification. As one of the protagonists clearly pointed out: "Little by little the wage pyramid will be reversed, and instead of having a wide base of unskilled labor with low salaries, that base will be reduced, and the number of jobs with higher wage opportunities will be increased through greater technical training and specialization."[6] For this, a policy of simple wage differentiation, and a more complex mechanism modifying the structure of remunerations in the industrial sector, were implemented. The weight of the basic salary for regular hours or overtime decreased, and the participation of other types of income, such as prizes and bonuses given for higher productivity, increased.[7]

What altered the historic tradition of uniform wages was the intensification of intersectoral differences. In Argentina, the wages of workers in similar categories or hierarchies were traditionally similar, regardless of the sector of activity to which these workers belonged. Union pressure, the state's populist wage policy, and the low negotiating capacity of employer organizations explained this pattern of equalization. But the power strategy of heterogenization, fragmentation and stratification of the popular classes fostered a great diversification of income among economic sectors. Table 7 clearly demonstrates this tendency to accentuate the differences of intersectoral remunerations in such a way, for example, that income in the banking sector was triple the average level of rural wages in 1976 and five times greater in 1980. Something similar occurs if one compares the different branches of manufacturing (although probably the tendency is more clear if one takes into account the levels of centralization of the branches or companies, but since there is no precise information on that point, we cannot arrive at any conclusion).

This wage stratification was associated with loss of economic power, because of the reduction in participation in the product on the part of industry and the deterioration of industrial wages, and the decreased participation by them in the value added of the sector.

If we consider that in the 1975–1982 period, in which the total gross domestic product (at factors cost) had an average annual growth rate lower than 1%, it is interesting to note that the financial sector grew more than 5%, agriculture less than 2%, and manufacturing dropped at an annual rate of 3%. The loss of the dynamic role played by industry becomes evident, as does the appearance of the financial sector, which tended to become the economic nucleus of the process. The former nuclear role of industrial activities linked with the production of durable consumer goods, especially in the automobile industry, and more generally, the fact that the industry as a whole was the dynamic nucleus of production, for years had given industrial workers and, more specifically, those in automobile and metal industries, a considerable economic power that translated into union strength and political leadership. But, during the period of the recent dictatorship, the dynamism of financial activities, the relevant role of finance capital in the articulation of mechanisms for the concentration of economic power, and the concurrent consequence of wage favoritism toward bank workers, reveals the possibility of a displacement of power roles in the popular sectors.

One of the most significant facts about this process of change in the classic homogeneity of the popular sectors based on the predominance of the wage laborers and, within them, of the working-class majority, is the reduction in the size of industrial labor. The number of workers in manufacturing (excluding administrative personnel, employers, partners and unpaid family members) was 1,165,000 in 1975, and it dropped to 740,000 in 1982, thus reducing in the same proportion these workers' social power, their aggregate weight, their negotiating capability, and their possibility of altering the existing relationships of force.

In the percentage structure by sectors of the active urban population, a reduction in industrial employment is also evident, as shown in Table 8. The data show the comprehensive decrease in the proportion of workers in the secondary sector (industry, electricity, construction and transportation): in 1974 they represented 48% of the active population, whereas in 1978 they were 44%. As this information deals only with urban activities, the primary sector does not appear here, even though we know from other sources that its size, too, had dropped. As for tertiary employment (commerce, finance, and services), it rose from 52% to 56% during that same period. This process of tertiarization in

Argentine society comes from the distant past, and it is caused by many factors but, in the present context, it represents a loss of social power by the industrial workers. As an element of the fragmentation of popular sectors, it is both the product of a disjunctive power strategy and of economic determinants.

9. As we can clearly observe in the information given in Table 9, the process of tertiarization of Argentina's global labor force—in the sense of a growing participation of employment in commerce, finance and services in the active population—goes back to the sixties. Between 1960 and 1970, these sectors grew from 33% of the economically active population to 41%. But during the years of the recent military dictatorship the process accelerated, and a qualitative change took place: in the main urban areas in which the Permanent Survey of Households gathered information (and including transport in the tertiary sector) the majority of the labor force belonged to the tertiary category by 1978. This can be inferred from the information in Table 8. A true social restructuration occurred in the popular sectors, which increased their fragmentation and converted industrial workers into a minority, thus debilitating their social power and scattering the support bases of their union action; this is a specific phenomenon that went beyond the normal tendencies of tertiarization in the capitalist world.

The effect of the restructuration of popular sectors, in the sense of channeling personnel from industry to services, of augmenting the number of employees to the detriment of workers, can be observed more clearly if one considers the absolute variations of employment by sector of the economy, and the participation of these sectors in the absorption or expulsion of workers. Table 9 shows the sudden drop in employment in manufacturing, which accounted for more than 90% of layoffs in the 1974–1978 period. At the same time, all the tertiary activities—in addition to construction—absorbed labor.

But what are these tertiary activities, and what is the purpose of pointing them out in the analysis? From Clark to Fourastié, classifications were established in terms of primary, secondary and tertiary employment. These distinctions were based on the kind of product generated by each, the consumer needs they satisfied, and the nature of the technological advances of each activity. The tertiary sector covered non-material production. But the problem of that classification is that it includes in the sector a heterogeneous mosaic of activities: commercial or financial circulation services (such as health, education, research, or recreation), and government. Theoretically it would be more correct to consider three great sectors (primary, secondary and tertiary) that would include basic activities (agricultural, industrial or services), and activities of finance and commerce as strictly linked in an intermediary manner to each basic sector.[8] In this way we would have primary production and circulation, secondary production and circulation, and something similar in the case of tertiary activity.

The relevance of these distinctions arises from the fact that they are associated with different forms of the organization of work, different characteristics of the work process, cultural traditions or differentiated forms of conscience, and variable styles of social struggle. The classification I propose, although more precise conceptually, is difficult to apply to available data, and for this reason I have presented these data on the basis of traditional groupings, accepting the existence of similarities between the processes of work in the activities of circulation in general and those of services.

Thus, the growing weight of employees in the occupational structure reveals their social power, and the economic dimension complements the image. According to the information contained in Table 5, tertiary activities—defined rather broadly therein—accounted for 50% of the Argentine domestic product in 1970 and for 52% in 1980. Of course that table incorrectly includes electricity in the tertiary sector and, in any case, the composition of the product is not an exhaustive indicator of the differential economic weight of the workers. In any event, it shows that these employees are connected with activities that account for more than half of the gross domestic product and this, even with the reservations I made, gives them considerable economic weight.

With regard to the political power of those in the tertiary, it is usual to point out the low level of combativeness of these sectors, their limited tradition of struggle, and the lack of cohesion derived from their insertion in a heterogeneous mosaic of differentiated activities. The low level of concentration in large enterprises, that permits the development of homogeneous union action and mechanisms of self-directed solidarity, brings about a low level of politically autonomous participation by tertiary employees, at least in comparison with industrial workers.[9]

An approximate indicator of the relative political power of the popular sectors is given by union membership and by the level of unionization. Since there are no recent data, I must go back to 1970. In Table 10 we can observe the dominant weight of the employee unions in the membership of the seventeen largest unions in Argentina: of these, more than half were in the tertiary sector. Teaching, retail, banking, government, and other smaller unions were the largest organizations in the nation. If it is considered that after 1970 and fundamentally during the recent military dictatorship there was a process of tertiarization, it is therefore probable that at present a greater modification has taken place in the correlation of union strength in favor of employees, and in detriment to workers.

But the sector of tertiary workers is not homogeneous. Beyond the presence of diverse branches of activity with different work processes and wage scales—as clearly shown in Table 7—this sector includes dissimilar forms of work organization: the state, the formal sector, and the informal one. The latter refers to intermittent workers, those working on their own account, and workers with low wages and precarious working conditions. The formal sector results from the dynamic requirements of material production and the investment of capital in services that respond to a growing demand. But both state services and the informal sector operate as areas of occupational shelter and with low wages, as indicated in Table 7.

10. The most obvious aspect of the process of heterogenization of the popular sectors, for it shows the workers excluded from wage relationships, is that of the growth of "independent" labor.

According to the information given in Table 4, in Argentine cities independent workers formed 19% of the active population in 1974 and 23% in 1978, which shows an accelerated growth. We know from the information in Tables 1 and 3 that Argentina traditionally had one of the highest levels of diffusion of wage labor in Latin America. Neither the peasant economy nor the work of artisans or other forms of autonomous employment played a significant role in the society. This gave to wage workers, and within that group, to industrial workers, a considerable weight. At present, independent workers form a contingent equivalent to that of workers in the manufacturing industry, the basic nucleus of the working class. Having a bearing on this development were the mechanism of subordinate reproduction, the economic crisis of the past few years and, fundamentally, the power strategy directed— by means of multiple molecular effects—toward the heterogenization, stratification and fragmentation of the popular sectors. The greater part of the expansion of independent employment originated in the layoff of wage industrial workers and flowed to tertiary activities, at least from 1974 to 1978.

As mentioned in a recent work, "the sectors that absorbed independent employment to a greater degree were services (some 60,000 persons) construction (44,000), commerce (37,000) and transport (6,000). They were responsible for keeping total employment constant, but also for the internal restructuring by employment categories."[10] Table 11, restricted to the largest Argentine cities, gives us a picture of the growth of independent employment, which rose to 24% in 1980. But it also permits us to visualize the greater rhythm of growth of independent employment in cities like Córdoba, Rosario and Mendoza, where, in addition to the general production crisis, were added the effects of an acute crisis of the regional economies. On the other hand, it is reasonable to assume that in the Argentine north independent work took on a more pronounced character of marginal, informal and precarious employment.

"Autonomous activity" is internally differentiated: it covers a work situation without wage labor that can be developed with an appreciable capital outlay which permits the appropriation of surplus; another in which independent workers without capital of any kind frequently show earnings lower than those of a stable wage worker; and an intermediate situation in which a small property-owner with low capital resources fails to appropriate surplus, and reproduces himself on the same scale. This variety of situations demonstrates the internal stratification of independent workers. But beyond that, together they have in common the fact of development of a non-socialized labor activity, on a small scale and with few technical resources, which links them to individualistic forms of social consciousness, with little tendency to collective union activity. Situated in the interstices of society, with limited economic power, due to their low productivity, organically disconnected from union activities that would energize their political strength, the independent workers, despite the social weight of their numbers, have objective interests not easily articulable with those of wage workers, or with the aggregate of popular sectors.

But the subproletarian situation of certain independent workers, that I characterized as self-employment without capital and with income levels lower than those of the stable wage workers, places us in contact with the problem of the forms of marginal employment. A power strategy of de-industrialization, channeled toward popular fragmentation and combined with an accelerated process of centralization of capital, of necessity tended to marginalize certain sectors of the population. Despite the expulsion of workers from neighboring countries, the emigration of Argentine manpower (basically professionals, technicians and skilled workers), and the decrease observed in the hours worked in industry, the shrinkage of productive employment determined the growth of the marginal forms of self-employment, the expansion of informal services, and, from 1980 on, increased unemployment and underemployment.

As can be seen in Table 12, the rate of open unemployment in the main cities of Argentina again shows the tendency toward a situation of structural unemployment. The rate of underemployment (those working less than 35 hours a week even though wanting to work more hours) in 1981 ranged from 5% (Greater Buenos Aires) to 13% (Mendoza). In 1982 it fluctuated from 9% (Greater Buenos Aires) to 12% (Mendoza), indicating a considerable increase—in relation to historic levels of visible underemployment. Thus the exacerbation of the presence of marginal sectors like those mentioned reveals another aspect of the fragmentation and weakening of popular strata that occurred during the dictatorial period.

11. I will now attempt to arrive at some general conclusions. I argued that the peculiar configuration of the social structure that gave rise—together with other factors—to the upsurge of popular movements in the first half of the seventies showed a heterogeneous social articulation at the top and a homogeneous one at the bottom. This was a situation that was slowly being transformed, owing to the Latin-Americanization of Argentine society, but which maintained its fundamental coordinates when the popular advances, prior to the takeover of 1976, occurred. Seen from this perspective, the economic failures of the dictatorship were transposed strangely into political successes, but meager and short-lived successes, because all that dislocating action of the rulers only served in the short term to hinder the workers' strength, and to prevent popular homogenization and its unified political expression. However, this power strategy has an aura of nostalgia. It does not offer any dynamic solutions to the grave economic and social problems of the nation, because it fails to project an image of development toward the future.

Obviously, the attempt to homogenize society from above brought about certain results, because the accelerated centralization concentrated economic power at the summit and erased the social power of numerous small and middle-level entrepreneurs, the traditional power base of populist projects. But the solution to the issue of hegemony was difficult, ephemeral and discordant: the finance sector entered a crisis, the productive sectors united against the "Patria financiera," as finance capital was popularly called, and the question is still alive today. Something similar but even graver occurred with the oligarchic dream of the conservative "military party" that would be the guarantor of order and the unifier of the dominant classes. Situated at the center of power, the military were traversed by the multiple contradictions of civil society and lost their specific function with the unfortunate episode of the Malvinas/Falkland Islands, after which they began to crumble. Needing to restructure itself as an institution, the military bureaucracy abandoned its party accouterments and retired to ensure control of its true sources of power: the barracks, arms, soldiers, in an attempt to restructure unifying hierarchies, standards, and values.

Popular fragmentation is the fundamental heritage left by this regressive social process. Labor stratification, de-industrialization, growth of sectors like the tertiary employees, the self-employed and the marginals, reveal a heterogenized, disjointed, and different popular life. This creates a challenge to the innovative capacity of the system's political actors. Moved by the choreography of power, the wage earners took a step backward to allow the advance of the self-employed and the marginal workers; within the wage earners' sector, the industrial workers moved backwards and employees came forward; this is a true movement of groups that radically altered the social sources of power and changed its economic bases, and modified the conditions of political action. But who are the social actors taking part in this dance? Workers, employees, independents, peasants, and marginal workers all appear as considerably heterogeneous figures, both in the sociological literature and in the chronicles of social struggle.

The projects of social change of the past century in European countries frequently presented industrial workers as the fundamental social subject; their context was the reality of growing industrial proletarization, high urbanization, and the constitution of industry as the connecting nucleus of the economic process. European rural rebellions in past centuries, as well as the wars of liberation in colonized societies, reveal a thread that shows the upsurge of the peasants (as the most notable figure in the different forms of independent labor) in the social struggles, with their concern for the land in fundamentally agricultural economies and their explosive forms of action. Marginality is associated with peasant poverty in Latin America, but in the Argentina of the military period it began to show itself as a mainly urban phenomenon, as industrial unemployment, as underemployment in services, as a precarious form of independent activity in circulation. Marginals do not seem to have been in history a social subject carrying projects of social change, but a force of social support for progressive as well as reactionary projects. But tertiary employees are perhaps the least studied, least known popular group, and the one that has become an absolute majority in Argentine popular sectors.

Argentina today is no longer a predominantly agricultural society, nor an industrial society, but rather one in which service activities have become predominant, and this brings about the consequent growth in the social power of employees. The labor about which the economy and society revolve in Argentina no longer is the manual labor of the earth, nor the mechanized labor of material production in industry, but rather the production of intangible services in which symbols are used for the production of symbols.

Bureaucrats, office workers, technicians, professionals, teachers, nurses, researchers, doctors, officials, salesmen, brokers, waiters, shoeshine boys, cashiers, etc., form a veritable army of workers who now are the majority of society; they represent a fragmented mosaic of activities diversely linked to the accumulation of capital, to the ideological reproduction of the system, and to the exercise of the lesser functions of power. Linked to different organizational forms of tertiary labor, like the work of government employees, the stable formal employment in the dynamic nuclei of circulation or services, and the informal employment in unstable street activities or marginal services, the tertiary employees manifest their real fragmentation behind the illusory mask of belonging to the category of wage workers. But, just as shown in Table 10, which sets forth the strength of unions in occupations such as teaching, retail, banking, governmental and others, their growing unionization, as well as the lower wage scales they receive—although there are some exceptions to this—and the specter of unemployment have converted the employees of Argentina into a blocked group, placed at a considerable distance from what might be called a "new petty bourgeoisie." At the present time, the characterization of employees in commerce, finance and services as a privileged class of society is more a myth than a concrete reality.

Finally, I will argue that the social changes analyzed as the heritage of the dictatorship, which leave in Argentine society deep changes in the social power of the actors, become a challenge to the political imagination of the popular sectors. At this point I may recall Gramsci when he says that the vitality of the parties is given by their capacity to react against the "spirit of routine." Perhaps the unexpected electoral results of 1983 and some symptoms of organic crisis observed in Argentine society might be some of the possible corollaries of the transformations analyzed. But those aspects suggest other fields of analysis; signals pointing out the path to be followed.

Notes

Translated by Mary Cooper.

1. See Michel Foucault, *Historia de la sexualidad* (Mexico: Siglo XXI, 1977), vol. 1, pp. 112–113.

2. Data from 1960 were taken initially in the preparation of these tables for it was in this decade that the process of worker radicalization and struggle, in their present specific forms, began.

3. See Raúl Sidicaro, "Poder y crisis de la gran burguesía agraria" in *Argentina, hoy,* ed. Alain Rouquié (Mexico: Siglo XXI, 1982).

4. See Pedro Paz, "Características de la gran expansión de la banca internacional privada" (Mexico: mimeograph, 1982).

5. See, for greater precision with regard to wage questions in the period being analyzed: J.M. Candia, "Argentina: apertura económica y mercado de trabajo" (M.A. thesis, UNAM Mexico, 1983). Other data that I present were taken from this work.

6. José A. Martínez de Hoz, in *El economista* (Buenos Aires), 5 January 1980.

7. According to data from INDEC (Instituto Nacional de Estadistica y Censos), the relative weight in the structure of industrial remunerations of "prizes, bonuses

and other items," went from 12% of total remuneration in 1975 to 22% in 1980. This was a suitable method of carrying out wage stratification by stimulating competition between the workers themselves.

8. The inclusion of service activities as a basic sector is due to the possibility that a privately appropriated surplus be generated in it, even though the realization of non-material goods justifies its distinction with respect to industrial and agricultural activities.

9. For differentiated levels of concentration and the forms of organization of tertiary workers, see Juan M. Villarreal, *Los asalariados en Argentina* (mimeograph, ENEP Acatlan, UNAM, 1980).

10. Ministerio de Trabajo. Dirección Nacional de Políticas y Programas Laborales, "El mercado de trabajo en Argentina" (Buenos Aires: 1980), p. 43.

Table 1.   Active Population in Some Countries around 1960 by Occupational Category

	Employers	Wage Workers	Independent Workers	Total
Argentina (1960)	13%	72%	15%	100%
Chile (1960)	2	76	22	100
Uruguay (1960)	9	74	17	100
Great Britain (1966)	2	93	5	100
Venezuela (1961)	3	61	36	100
Brazil (1960)	2	48	40	100
Mexico (1960)	1	64	35	100
Ecuador (1962)	2	49	49	100

Source: National Population Censuses.

Note: The "unspecified" category has been eliminated, and "self-employed" and "family employed" have been included under the category of "independents," since they do not express wage relations. The same procedure has been carried out in Table 3.

Table 2.   Distribution of the Active Population in Some Countries around 1960 by Sectors of Activity

	Agriculture	Industry	Services	Total
Argentina	20%	36%	44%	100%
United States	7	36	57	100
Brazil	52	15	33	100
Mexico	55	20	25	100

Source: World Bank, 1979.

Table 3.   Active Population in Some Countries around 1970 by Occupational Category

	Employers	Wage Workers	Independent Workers	Total
Argentina (1970)	6%	73%	21%	100%
Great Britain (1966)	2	93	5	100
Mexico (1970)	6	62	32	100
Ecuador (1962)	2	49	49	100
Venezuela (1970)	3	67	30	100
United States (1970)	2	87	11	100
Uruguay (1963)	9	74	17	100
Honduras (1970)	3	62	35	100

Source: National Population Censuses.

Table 4.   Active Population in Argentine Urban Areas by Occupational Category

	1974	1978
Employers	4.6%	3.4%
Wage Workers	68.9	66.1
Self-employed	18.8	22.6
Others	7.7	7.9
Total	100.0	100.0

Source: INDEC (Instituto Nacional de Estadistica y Censos), Permanent Household Survey.

Note: In this table, as opposed to Tables 1 and 3, the self-employed are taken separately, and family members and "unspecified" are included in "others."

Table 5.   Sectoral Evolution of the GDP in Argentina

	1970	1975	1980
Agriculture, hunting and fishing	12.9%	12.9%	12.9%
Mines and quarries	2.2	2.1	2.5
Manufactures	28.0	28.6	25.4
Construction	6.4	5.8	7.6
Services, commerce and finance	50.4	50.6	51.7
Total	100.0	100.0	100.0

Source: FIDE (Fundación de Investigaciones para el Desarrollo Económico) based on data from the Central Bank, May 1981.

Note: The sector of services, commerce and finance includes activities such as electricity and transport.

Table 6:   Index of Man-hours in Manufacturing
(Second Quarters. Index 1970 = 100)

Sector	1971	1972	1973	1974	1975	1976
Foodstuffs	107.2	113.6	107.4	121.9	125.6	125.6
Beverages	97.4	101.7	107.9	117.9	129.5	119.0
Tobacco	109.7	108.9	106.8	125.3	144.7	154.3
Textiles	112.3	108.0	102.9	117.6	128.3	116.4
Clothing	102.9	106.7	158.6	117.0	119.9	112.6
Hides	103.2	124.7	134.9	149.1	147.3	150.6
Shoes	103.4	89.6	94.2	104.5	104.7	88.8
Lumber and derivatives	102.5	101.2	98.9	97.3	129.6	149.3
Furniture and accessories	100.1	94.3	95.5	96.1	89.7	73.8
Paper and derivatives	104.0	117.8	113.1	111.1	121.6	117.9
Printing and publishing	99.9	102.3	104.3	107.1	113.1	98.0
Industrial chemical substances	100.8	111.8	110.2	112.6	121.5	129.4
Other chemical products	106.6	104.5	101.6	104.5	108.9	108.9
Petroleum refineries	105.6	119.4	120.7	124.1	139.6	147.3
Petroleum and coal derivatives	86.4	91.2	96.7	88.4	93.9	105.8
Rubber products	114.0	123.8	123.1	143.0	148.7	139.9
Plastic products	102.8	157.2	198.7	190.3	202.2	186.1
Clay, china and porcelain	116.0	126.2	125.1	113.2	119.8	123.6
Glass and derivatives	101.7	116.3	112.9	109.7	120.4	117.9
Non-metallic mining	103.7	103.8	97.7	102.8	105.8	104.6
Basic iron and steel industries	107.0	124.8	135.7	134.5	126.3	134.2
Basic non-ferrous metal industries	134.3	145.5	154.3	140.7	153.9	147.6
Metallic products	111.6	114.3	120.0	131.8	125.2	119.9
Non-electric machinery	103.0	103.4	108.6	117.4	117.4	113.0
Electric machinery and appliances	108.2	109.8	105.0	109.2	102.2	89.0
Transportation equipment	107.7	115.6	115.9	128.0	135.8	134.3
Professional equipment	112.4	121.9	131.8	157.4	158.9	162.4
General Level	106.5	109.3	111.4	118.7	122.9	120.0

Source: INDEC (Instituto Nacional de Estadística y Censos).

Table 6.   Index of Man-hours in Manufacturing (continued)
(Second Quarters. Index 1970 = 100)

Sector	1977	1978	1979	1980	1981
Foodstuffs	125.0	117.9	120.8	112.1	108.0
Beverages	111.2	109.0	104.8	116.7	108.8
Tobacco	112.6	103.6	105.2	109.7	137.0
Textiles	113.7	98.5	98.0	73.0	58.9
Clothing	95.5	94.0	83.2	65.5	57.1
Hides	183.7	161.4	157.1	117.5	93.7
Shoes	84.0	60.1	60.8	57.2	53.5
Lumber and derivatives	134.6	114.1	102.1	93.3	74.8
Furniture and accessories	61.6	59.1	58.9	67.0	68.5
Paper and derivatives	119.7	124.5	125.3	101.6	91.7
Printing and publishing	84.5	80.0	83.0	93.9	84.4
Industrial chemical substances	122.5	108.5	105.9	105.3	84.7
Other chemical products	99.7	90.8	89.0	88.8	77.6
Petroleum refineries	145.5	150.0	130.8	119.3	119.9
Petroleum and coal derivatives	88.0	96.2	89.4	80.8	84.5
Rubber products	143.7	124.8	149.6	137.8	160.7
Plastic products	151.4	133.0	145.4	153.6	128.2
Clay, china and porcelain	103.3	90.1	116.5	113.0	75.7
Glass and derivatives	112.0	127.1	108.8	99.5	74.2
Non-metallic mining	101.1	94.9	96.8	92.4	84.6
Basic iron and steel industries	134.8	119.5	124.1	124.4	94.5
Basic non-ferrous metal industries	153.4	138.9	147.3	139.3	125.9
Metallic products	117.2	106.1	114.8	104.9	83.7
Non-electric machinery	111.8	100.0	96.0	78.0	51.9
Electric machinery and appliances	93.3	80.2	85.0	83.0	62.7
Transportation equipment	136.0	101.3	113.5	116.2	91.8
Professional equipment	146.7	140.0	149.9	105.9	84.7
General Level	116.8	104.1	106.2	98.5	83.9

Source: INDEC (Instituto Nacional de Estadística y Censos).

Table 7.   Wage Differentiation among Sectors of Economic Activity in Argentina
(Index Numbers. Base = General Level of the Year)

	1976	1980
Industry	107.5	107.8
Commerce	110.7	100.9
Banks	128.3	175.3
Automotive transport	80.6	83.1
Rural	43.4	34.6
Central administration	69.2	77.6
Government enterprises	128.2	147.6
Remainder (special wage scales)	98.1	131.3
General level	100.0	100.0

Source: Permanent Wage Survey, Ministry of Social Action, Buenos Aires, 1981.

Table 8.   Employed Personnel in Argentine Urban Areas by Sector

Sectors	1974	1976	1978
Manufacturing	32.5%	29.7%	28.5%
Electricity and others	1.2	1.2	1.0
Construction	6.8	7.4	7.9
Transport and communications	7.0	6.9	6.8
Commerce	17.8	18.6	18.8
Finance and others	4.1	4.7	5.2
Services	30.6	31.4	31.8
Total	100.0	100.0	100.0

Source: INDEC (Instituto Nacional de Estadistica y Censos), Permanent Household
Survey.

Table 9.   Variations in Employed Manpower in Urban Areas of Argentina, 1974-1978

	In Thousands Employed	Sector Participation in the Layoffs of Employed Personnel, in Percentages
Manufacturing	-181	-91.0
Electricity	- 7	- 3.5
Construction	+ 53	+26.6
Commerce	+ 44	+22.1
Transport	- 11	- 5.5
Finance	+ 47	+23.6
Services	+ 55	+27.6

Source: FIDE (Fundación de Investigaciones para el Desarrollo Económico), based
on information from the Ministry of Labor.

Table 10: Union Membership in 1970 (Seventeen Largest Unions)

		No.	%
1. Confederación de Trabaja- dores de la Educación	Teachers	220,000	14.6
2. Unión obrera Metalúrgica	Metalworkers	180,000	11.9
3. Confederación General de Empleados de Comercio	Commerce	171,000	11.3
4. Unión Ferroviaria	Railroads	168,978	11.2
5. Asociación Obrera Textil	Textiles	115,000	7.6
6. Asociación Bancaria	Banking	77,620	5.1
7. Unión Obrera de la Con- strución	Construction Construction	75,000	4.9
8. Asociación Trabajadores del Estado	Government	70,000	4.6
9. Unión Obreros y Empleados Municipales de Capital Federal	Muncipal Workers, Buenos Aires	65,000	4.3
10. Obreros y Empleados Muni- cipales de Avellaneda	Municipal Workers, Avellaneda	56,884	3.8
11. Unión Trabajadores Gastronómicos	Waiters	56,500	3.7
12. Federación Arg. de Traba- jadores de Luz y Fuerza	Electricity	53,286	3.5
13. Unión del Personal Civil de la Nación	Government	50,100	3.3
14. Federación Obrera Nacional de la Industria del Vestido y Afines	Garment	43,000	2.8
15. Sindicato de Mecánicos y Afines del Transporte Automotor	Automotive	40,000	2.6
16. Federación Argentina de Trabajadores de la Sanidad	Health	38,267	2.5
17. Federación Obreros y Empleados Telefónicos	Telephone	30,009	2.0
Total Membership		1,510,644	100.0

Sources: INDEC (Instituto Nacional de Estadística y Censos) and CGT (Confederación General del Trabajo).

Table 11. Proportion of Self-employed Workers in Relation to the Active Population of the Main Cities of Argentina

	(October of each year)			
	1974	1976	1978	1980
Greater Buenos Aires	18.5%	20.1%	22.5%	23.1%
Córdoba	18.1	23.7	26.5	28.4
Mendoza	21.6	23.8	23.7	27.8
Rosario	20.8	24.2	24.4	26.7
Santa Fe	17.7	33.9	24.5	22.8
Tucumán	17.2	18.9	17.9	18.2
Total	18.8	20.6	22.6	23.8

Source: INDEC (Instituto Nacional de Estadistica y Censos), Permanent Household Survey.

Table 12. Unemployment Rates in Argentina

Jurisdiction	April							
	1974	1975	1976	1977	1978	1979	1980	1981
Greater Buenos Aires	4.2	2.4	4.8	3.4	3.9	2.0	2.3	3.9
Córdoba	7.0	6.1	6.5	5.9	5.1	2.6	2.1	2.9
Rosario	4.6	5.3	5.3	3.5	5.5	3.1	4.3	4.8
Tucumán	10.6	8.4	7.4	7.3	6.8	5.9	6.2	7.3
Mendoza	4.9	4.1	5.9	4.4	2.9	2.8	1.4	4.1

Source: FIDE (Fundación de Investigaciones para el Desarrollo Económico), based on data from INDEC (Instituto Nacional de Estadistica y Censos).

5

The Legitimation of Democracy Under Adverse Conditions: The Case of Argentina

Carlos H. Waisman

The transition from military rule to liberal democracy in Argentina is taking place under three unfavorable conditions.[1]

In the first place, the Alfonsín administration inherited an economy in a deep crisis. The economic legacy of the military regime is a combination of stagnation, hyper-inflation, and high indebtedness. The policies of that regime were a reflection of its incoherence: trade liberalization and unrestrained spending, an explosive mix in a society with a non-competitive manufacturing sector and a highly organized and mobilized working class. Stagnation or, more properly, retrogression, was the first consequence: from 1975 to 1983, the per capita GDP grew at an average annual rate of .3%, but in 1980–1983 it declined at a rate of 4.3%.[2] The contraction was especially strong in manufacturing: from 1976 to 1982, industrial GDP per capita fell by more than 20%.[3] Hyper-inflation was another by-product: when Alfonsín came to power, at the end of 1983, inflation was running at the three-digit level, and it reached 400% in the first quarter of 1984. Finally, the Argentine debt, which stood at over 40 billion in 1983 and now is over 50 billion, is the third largest in Latin America, but it is higher in relation to exports than those of Brazil or Mexico.

Secondly, it is true that the military regime fell because consent to it collapsed, as a consequence of the defeat in the Malvinas-Falklands War with Britain, the economic catastrophe, and the massive violations of human rights; but the institutional infrastructure of authoritarianism and corporatism was not broken. The country still had a partially autonomous state apparatus, strong interest groups, and weak political parties.

The military may have lost their legitimacy as a player in the mass praetorian game, but large segments of the armed forces and of the intelligence apparatus whose tentacles penetrate every area of Argentine society still saw themselves, when the new government came to power, as independent from the government, as exempt from subordination to the law, as endowed with the privilege to define the national interest, and with the prerogative to be the central organs for the protection of such interest. Small but significant circles within these organizations still had ties with clandestine para-military cells, extreme right-wing groups, and possibly even criminal elements. On the side of interest groups, trade union leaders with corporatist inclinations and business elites that traditionally opted for military solutions still controlled large and powerful organizations. Finally, neither of the two large parties, Radicals and Peronists, had a substantial control of interest group organizations.

Third, liberal democratic traditions are weak in Argentina, after half a century of political instability, military dictatorships, populist-corporatist governments, and exclusionary democracies. The espousal of democratic principles by the major political forces was always conditional and limited. Before the Depression, the agrarian elite and the Conservatives were more committed to the toleration of dissent than to the extension of participation to the rest of society, even though they eventually did integrate the middle classes into the political system. After the Depression, the agrarians and their party were central supporters of non-democratic regimes. As for the middle classes and the Radical party, they had a stronger commitment to constitutional rule up to World War II, but they later supported restrictive regimes that excluded Peronism and labor. Peronists, finally, espoused majority rule, but their commitment to toleration of dissent and to political freedoms was always contingent.

These three adverse conditions were, to some extent, balanced by two factors conducive to democratization. The first was the de-legitimation of non-democratic formulae, and consequently a shift toward moderation and compromise among all the major social and political forces. Specific political regimes are organized into codes, which vary from society to society and from sector to sector within each society. The legitimacy of any political regime, be it established or just a theoretical possibility, is a function of the legitimacy of its alternatives. The range of these alternatives varies, according to the direct experience different groups and societies had with specific regimes, and also to the indirect experience acquired through demonstration effects to which different societies and groups within each society may have had access.

In Argentina, all the alternatives to liberal democracy considered reasonable and acceptable by the major social forces have been tried, and they have failed: exclusionary democracy, corporatist-populist regimes, "soft" military rule, highly coercive military rule. Even the socialist option, espoused by a sector of the intelligentsia, has lost its glamour: in terms of direct experience, there is consensus that the "military road" tried in the sixties and seventies led to disaster; in terms of indirect experiences, neither the "peaceful road" attempted in Chile under Allende nor the successful socialist experiences in Latin America, Europe, or Asia arouse mass support. None of the other available non-democratic models in the world today are considered by significant groups in the society as options worth following.

As a consequence, liberal democracy enjoys substantial legitimacy, largely by default. Because all the other plausible roads have been followed with negative results, Argentines are re-discovering the virtues of pluralism and toleration of dissent. To some extent, liberal democracy is a road not tried: its principles were, in the experience of all but the older Argentines, empty formulae enshrined in a systematically violated constitution. The parties that in the Orwellian language of Argentine politics are called "liberal" maintained in the past decades at most a theoretical support for political liberalism, but they were prompt, or willing, according to the circumstances, to re-define liberal formulae as abstract ideals, not applicable to Argentine reality. Peronists and other so-called "national" groups were not so hypocritical: they never espoused the principles of liberal democracy, but after the prolonged experience of exclusion and intolerance some sectors in this camp perceived the benefits of a political arrangement in which the opponent is not a foe to be destroyed.

The second circumstance conducive to democratization is the fact that the Alfonsín administration and the Radical Party are committed to the institutionalization of the two dimensions of liberal democracy: participation as well as contestation. Such commitment would not have been categorically present had the Peronists won the 1983 elections. The majority of the Radical leadership supports the conventional forms of competitive politics, but some sectors experience the "movementist" pull that David Rock discusses elsewhere in this volume, and propose the formation of a "third historic movement." The nature of this movement is still unclear (an enlarged Radical party, a new party, a front?), but its ideology and expected social base are more definite. The ideology would combine political liberalism and moderately populist and nationalist economic policies, and the social base would incorporate a segment of the working class. As of this writing (end of 1985), the propounders of this road are losing ground. In any case, the project deserves some attention, given its affinity with past arrangements. The impact of such a movement on the prospects for democratization would depend on the eventual characteristics of the party system. The formation of a Mexican-style hegemonic party would obviously not be conducive to the institutionalization of competitive democracy. A coalition involving Radicals and Peronists as distinct parties, on the other hand, would not hinder democratization. Under certain conditions, it could be the most effective mechanism for the implementation of economic policies favorable for the consolidation of democracy, an issue to which I will return.

These democratic orientations in the ruling party and in the major social forces can sustain the process of legitimation, but they may weaken as the different groups pursue their interests: the adverse economic, political, and cultural factors listed above may eventually block the transition. The reason is that there is a structural cause of mass praetorianism, namely the fact that Argentina combines an economy in which a large proportion of labor and capital are committed to non-competitive manufacturing with a society having highly mobilized and organized social forces. The surplus generated by agrarian exports has been to a considerable extent appropriated by the state and channeled toward an industrial sector whose size in terms of share of GDP and of the labor force is comparable to those of advanced capitalist nations, but which developed behind tariff and non-tariff barriers that are among the highest in the world. This hot-house capitalism led, as could be expected, given the size of the Argentine market, to atrophy as soon as this market was saturated. Diversification and "deepening" efforts led to temporary spurts, but the long-term trend has been toward low growth rates.

On the other hand, Argentine society has high levels of political mobilization and strong interest groups. The working class, in particular, is highly unionized, and the labor movement, in the decades prior to the establishment of the latest military regime, was based on large, unified, and relatively affluent organizations. Up to the seventies, unions had a high level of control of the labor market. This was a function of a historical peculiarity of Argentina: the fact that the country lacked a substantial peasantry, and that it had a population shortage for most of its history.[4] The existence of such a strong working class, and also of a large and mobilized middle class, in the near-stagnated economy Argentina had for most of the past three decades, goes a long way toward explaining why post-Peronist Argentina was the perfect embodiment of mass praetorianism, in Huntington's sense.

Argentine society has changed in the seventies as a consequence of the processes described by Michael P. Monteón, Monica Peralta-Ramos, and Juan M. Villarreal elsewhere in this volume: the industrial bourgeoisie was transformed by the concentration and centralization of capital in some sectors and the decline and massive bankruptcy in others, the strength of labor declined as a product of de-industrialization and repression, and the different segments of the informal sector grew. The correlation of forces was transformed by the weakening of the social base of Peronism, but this does not imply that the structural determinants of polarization and instability have disappeared. This would be tantamount to blaming labor for the political illegitimacy of the post-Peronist period. The sources of instability, as I pointed out, are to be found in this coexistence of a low-growth or stagnated economy and a society with highly mobilized and organized social forces. Labor may be weaker, but it is still a major power contender. So are the different strata of the middle class, and the different fractions of the bourgeoisie. And we still know little about the mobilization potential of the informal sector.

The intensity of this structural threat is aggravated by the new factor, the large foreign debt. In most of the post-Peronist period, the different social forces contended for the surplus in the context of an economy that fluctuated cyclically. This allowed for the pattern of sequential satisfaction, to some extent, of the basic interests of the most powerful groups. From now on, the Argentine economy is likely to remain in a state of protracted stagnation, as a large share of the gains from agrarian exports is allocated to the service of the debt. There is a clear danger, then, that the destabilization mechanism that destroyed elected governments in the past could be activated again. This destabilization mechanism is well known: balance of payment difficulties forced governments to carry out recessionary policies; these triggered the intense mobilization of labor and other social forces, and this mobilization led to runaway-inflation and high levels of polarization; the outcome was panic among the bourgeoisie and segments of the middle class, government paralysis, and a military coup aimed at re-establishing "order" through social demobilization.

The institutionalization of democracy presupposes two processes: the weakening of the institutional infrastructure of authoritarianism and corporatism, and the display of at least a modest degree of efficacy by the new political institutions.

The first of these processes, in turn, involves changes in the state and in the party system. The state apparatus, the military and the security and intelligence organizations in particular, must be placed under government control; and a system of parties which are strong vis-a-vis interest groups and also committed to the rules of the democratic game should develop. Since the Radical Party can be reasonably expected, in the absence of very high levels of social polarization, to meet these requirements, the problem is whether a democratic opposition is likely to develop. Neither a party system based on two major parties nor the survival of Peronism as the largest opposition are pre-ordained, but the situation as of the end of 1985 indicates that these are the most reasonable assumptions for the near future. The question becomes, then, whether Peronism is likely to become a strong opposition party committed to liberal democracy.

As for the need for some efficacy, the issue is the classical one posed by Lipset, Linz, Blondel, and others: in order to be legitimate, a regime must meet, to some degree, the needs of its citizens. This requirement is, of course, most pressing for newly established regimes, which cannot bank on past performance. Economic efficacy, in particular, is strategically important.[5] It can be argued that there are non-economic aspects of performance that have causal weight: a government may satisfy people's needs through different types of social reform that do not require economic growth. Moreover, and this is very important in post-authoritarian situations, the experience of democracy is in itself a manifestation of efficacy and therefore it has legitimating consequences, regardless of whether democracy is accompanied by greater material welfare.

It is undeniable, however, that some degree of economic efficacy, and hence of economic growth, even if not immediate, is necessary for the legitimation of the new regime, especially after a protracted period of stagnation and retrogression. The problem in the Argentine case is that the resumption of long-term economic growth presupposes structural reform, basically the development of some manufactures with an export potential, and this in turn requires the reconversion of a segment of the non-competitive industrial sector.

Thus, the consolidation of liberal democracy can only be an aspect of a larger process, whose essence is the unmaking of the wrong choices made in the forties. I have argued that the coup of 1943 and the successor Peronist regime transformed the previous pattern of economic and political development of Argentina, by turning the state downward and the economy inward.[6] In order to unblock its economy and reconstitute a legitimate political system at the same time, the country must return to open industrialization and institutionalize competitive politics.

The issues are, then, the subordination of the autonomous areas of the state to the government, the evolution of Peronism, and the prospects for reconversion. The extent to which outcomes favorable to the process of democratization occur will depend to a considerable degree on how the government manages these questions. Over-all, the performance of the Alfonsín administration in this regard has been mixed so far, but significant steps in the right direction have been taken.

As far as the first issue is concerned, the government has no choice. It must proceed fast and take full control of the military and security apparatus. Paradoxically, it is in this area, which was intractable for two generations, that the administration has the best chances for success. The reason is, of course, the loss of whatever legitimacy the armed forces had as an independent political actor.

In the beginning of the new government, some measures aimed at reducing the power of the military and placing them under civilian control. Many top officers were retired, the defense budget was substantially reduced, and many of the non-military firms and agencies controlled by the armed forces were removed from their jurisdiction. The government also endeavored to harness the intelligence agencies, and to dismantle para-military groups and outlaw gangs attached to the security apparatus.

The handling of human rights violations was the thorniest issue in the relationship between the new government and the armed forces. Human rights organizations, which are supported mainly by the left, are led by a small stratum of highly dedicated activists, many of whom are relatives of victims of repression. Their demands were basically two: the trial of all officers implicated in the kidnapping, torture, illegal imprisonment, and killing of real or imagined opponents of the regime, and the handling of these cases by civilian courts. The official position of the military was, on the other hand, that the armed forces had not committed any crimes: there had been a war, and those who died had fallen in combat. Even after irrefutable evidence to the contrary surfaced, the military establishment maintained that there had not been a "Gulag" of illegal detention centers, and that no killings in non-combat situations had taken place.

Government policy tried to steer a course between these two positions. Its goal was to induce the armed forces to punish the major offenders, thereby protecting the officer corps and restoring some legitimacy to the institution. On the government's initiative, the newly established Congress repealed the "amnesty" that the military had declared for themselves, and it passed a law establishing that charges against officers would be heard by military judges, but there would be a review by civilian courts. The government also appointed a blue-ribbon commission, which gathered evidence about the "disappeared."[7] Finally, in order to appease the officer corps, the administration formulated a very questionable doctrine, according to which only those who gave illegal orders and those who violated the law on their own initiative should be prosecuted. Therefore, soldiers who breached the law while obeying orders would not be considered responsible, even if these orders involved manifest transgressions of the law.

In spite of its moderation, the government's strategy did not succeed. Its underlying assumption was that officers would behave as individual rational maximizers, and thus they would realize that accepting Alfonsín's policy was the most effective way to further their bureaucratic careers and to increase the prestige of the armed forces. Instead, the bulk of the military establishment closed ranks in a silent but still challenging manner, which reveals both the prevalence of individual fear to the revision of the past and the survival of an esprit-de-corps which in fact is a conception of the armed forces as an entity independent of the government and placed above the law.

The administration ordered the members of the military juntas tried for human rights violations. The defendants were cleared by military judges, in spite of the overwhelming evidence against them. But the cases were reviewed by civilian courts, and most leaders of the military regime were convicted, two of them to life. Before the verdicts were issued, a wave of bombings took place, forcing the government to resort to the state of siege. A right-wing terrorist cell, made up of a few officers on active duty—one of whom had a high position in the intelligence apparatus—and right-wing politicians was discovered and de-activated. However, there was no institutional resistance by the armed forces, and the former dictators are now in jail. A handful of other notorious criminals is being tried, and this is likely to be the full extent of judicial redress. There is even talk in official circles of some kind of amnesty, that would protect lower-rank officers in a categorical manner. In any case, the defendants at these trials were not just the former leaders of the military regime, but the armed forces as a whole. Their passive acceptance of the trials may simply be due to the absence of support by any major social force, but it could also mark the beginning of a process of forced subordination of the military to civilian rule. Herein lies the significance of these trials: it is the first time since the onset of military intervention in 1930 that subversive officers must answer for their actions before a court of law. From now on, conspirators must reckon with the demonstration affect of these verdicts.

The problem is that the structure and doctrine of the armed forces has not changed. As long as the military continue being a large and unwieldy organization geared to the control of the domestic population and run on the basis of variants of the "national security doctrine," a central ingredient of the institutional infrastructure of authoritarianism will be in place. The need for a radical restructuration of the services involving educational reform, reductions in size, changes in the patterns of organization and deployment, and a new doctrine of "national defense," is recognized by government officials, but policy changes are still under discussion. Time is of the essence here, for the government must act while the memory of the military regime is still fresh and the level of polarization in the society is not high. Thorough military reform may prove more difficult in the future, if economic difficulties lead to mass mobilization by labor and the middle classes and to a decline of support for the Alfonsín administration.

The key to the dismantling of the institutional infrastructure of authoritarianism and corporatism lies, however, with another ingredient: Peronism and the unions. If they are thoroughly integrated into the democratic system, constitutional rule could be strengthened even in the absence of a full reform of the armed forces. This leads us to the second issue, i.e., the prospects for the transformation of Peronism into a political organization strong vis-a-vis the unions and committed to liberal democracy, and more generally the outlook for the institutionalization of a democratic opposition.

Peronism lost the 1983 election as a consequence of several factors: its fragmentation, the decline of its labor wing as a consequence of de-industrialization and repression, the memories of its disastrous performance in 1973–1976, the passive assent that a segment of it had given to the 1976 coup, and the leadership crisis that followed Perón's death. Accurately, many voters perceived the Peronist establishment as an organic part of the authoritarian-corporatist bloc (what Alfonsín called the "military-union pact"). In addition, the Peronist labor movement was weakened by the questionable legitimacy of many of its leaders, whose tenure in office had been extended without elections during the military regime.

The new government tried to avoid two extremes in its relationship with the unions: tactical accommodation with the existing leadership, and all-out war against it. The first option would have been expedient in the short run, but it would have left one of the pillars of corporatism intact. The second road, given the strength of Peronism and the fact that a recession was almost inevitable, would have led to an early activation of the destabilizing mechanism described above. In order to democratize the labor movement, the government sent Congress a bill mandating court-controlled union elections, and establishing minority representation in union government. The Peronist-controlled Senate rejected this bill, and eventually the Radicals accepted a milder alternative: elections organized by the existing leadership and on the basis of existing union constitutions, which usually do not provide for minority representation in the top governing bodies. The outcome was unexpectedly negative for the established leaders. Many of them remained in office, but they lost control of important organizations as non-machine Peronists,

Radicals, and some leftists made significant inroads. The overall trend is toward a more pluralistic labor movement, in which right-wing Peronists will be a significant force but not the hegemonic one.

As for the behavior of the labor movement vis-a-vis the government, it has been quite restrained. The stabilization policy followed in the second half of 1985 has caused a significant drop in real wages, and there is widespread anxiety about the rise of unemployment and the growth of the informal sector. There have been some important strikes, including some general ones, and isolated factory takeovers, but the overall level of labor mobilization was so far lower than in past situations in which labor faced adverse economic conditions in a context that permitted oppositional political action. This restraint is the consequence of the overall process of moderation in all major social forces I noted above, and of the high level of collective insecurity produced by the recent experiences of de-industrialization and by the concern about rising unemployment. The efficacy of these barriers to mobilization could lessen as the deterioration of standards of living continues (a likely occurrence), for the political conditions of liberal democracy are conducive to the formation of a large stratum of activists, who could persuade workers to re-interpret their experience in ways conducive to mobilization.

As for Peronism as a political party, it entered a profound crisis after the defeat of 1983. As electoral support decreased (40 percent in 1983, 34 percent in 1985), internal fragmentation intensified. Alongside the traditional leadership, oriented toward corporatism and populist forms of authoritarianism, a moderate or "Renovator" wing inclined toward the acceptance of liberal democracy grew in all districts, and captured the party organization in many of them. The two segments presented separate slates in the last congressional election, and the right was reduced to insignificance in many provinces.

Peronism is still, however, far from being a democratic opposition party. The anti-democratic right controls important organizations (including the largest one, the Province of Buenos Aires), and leaders of major unions are its potential allies. For Peronism to turn into a stabilizing opposition party representing its constituencies, labor and the urban poor in the core regions of the country and broader coalitions in the periphery, it should develop a strong but pluralistic organization, and an ideology that accepts political liberalism.

The prospects for such transformation will be enhanced if support for the government remains high, if pressures from below for labor mobilization against recessionary policies are moderate, and if the Left does not make significant inroads in the unions. A high level of support for the Alfonsín administration would strengthen the democratic segment of Peronism by making it obvious to all groups in the movement that loyal opposition to the Radicals is the strategy most likely to pay off in terms of electoral support, given the new political culture, the widespread dissatisfaction with the economic situation, and the high potential cost of destabilizing alternatives. Pressures from below could trigger a militant offensive that would push Peronism toward a destabilizing type of opposition: just the perception by union activists that grievances are so intense that conditions for mobilization exist could trigger such an outcome, for competing groups of activists would have a powerful incentive to induce mobilization in order to pre-empt each other. Finally, a substantial growth of the radical Left in the labor movement (either the Communist Party or the MAS, Movement toward Socialism) would spur a two-pronged response by the established leadership: direct attempts to repress or expel the Left on the one hand and, as in the case of anticipated pressures from below, pre-emptive mobilization of the rank and file on the other.

These three conditions favorable to the transformation of Peronism into a social-democratic party would all be manifestations of the process still underway, the trend toward moderation and pragmatism in different sectors of Argentine society. The question is how long will this trend last: the real incomes of workers and large segments of the middle classes have fallen considerably since the re-establishment of democracy, and prospects for growth are bleak in the absence of structural changes in the Argentine economy.

In the first year of the new administration, economic policy focused on the debt negotiation. The antagonists the government faced were the International Monetary Fund, the major lending banks, and the governments of lending nations, the U.S. in particular. The Alfonsín government endeavored to follow a middle road between two extreme and unacceptable options: an orthodox, IMF-style stabilization program, and a unilateral moratorium or the like. The government was aware that the first alternative would trigger a high level of polarization, and that the second one would disrupt international trade, cut the country off from international finance, and eventually lead to an even more serious explosion.

The government aimed for a compromise with the Fund and the banks that would allow for gradual adjustments, while domestic policy endeavored to maintain real wages and employment levels. Inflation, fueled by wage indexing and by government spending, reached the four-digit level in early 1985. The critical situation forced the government to shift toward stabilization policies, the "Austral Plan." In mid-1985, the currency was changed and prices and wages were frozen, the administration promised to stop the unbacked issue of money (a truly revolutionary measure), reduce the deficit, and maintain stable exchange rates. There are also plans to privatize some firms in the huge and inefficient public sector.

These policies had immediate positive effects: inflation was reduced to manageable levels, debt negotiations shifted from confrontational to co-operative bargaining, and the country is even likely to attract some capital (both foreign investment and domestic capital sent abroad). The Austral Plan will not deal, however, with the central structural problem of the Argentine economy: the dualism between the competitive agrarian sector and the non-competitive manufacturing one.

As I pointed out above, the development of export manufactures requires, in the current Argentine context, at least a partial reconversion of the existing industrial sector, for the growth of a substantial competitive segment alongside the existing non-competitive one is not likely in the short or medium term, for at least two reasons. First, a large-scale inflow of foreign capital is not to be expected in a country without non-renewable or strategic raw materials, with a relatively small domestic market, a highly mobilized working class, and a history of political instability. Second, domestic resources for the importation of machinery and other inputs will not be available, in the face of the need to service the debt, the unlikely rise of prices for Argentina's traditional exports, and the rigid import requirements of existing industry.

Since reconversion would affect the interests of the major social forces in the society—the industrial bourgeoisie, labor, and segments of the middle classes linked to them—its implementation is a major risk for any political regime, more so for a regime that depends on the consent of the governed, and much more so for a newly established one. And yet reconversion is, in my view, the key to the re-establishment of a "virtuous" relationship between Argentina and the international economy, and thus one of the pre-conditions for the institutionalization of liberal democracy.

A policy of industrial reconversion need not have the catastrophic effects that the lowering of tariffs and the overvaluation of the currency had in the late seventies. As was then the case, blanket tariff cuts and the reliance on Darwinian mechanisms would lead to another wave of bankruptcies and layoffs, and thus to very high levels of polarization. A policy of gradual or segmented transformation, on the other hand, could have positive economic results, and it would be feasible in the current Argentine situation. Such a policy would identify sectors to be dismantled and sectors with an export potential. Some of the latter may exist already, while others have to be started. Reconversion would take place in stages, and any lowering of tariffs should be accompanied by policies that would cushion its impact: financial support for the acquisition of new technology, programs for the re-training of labor, etc.

At the political level, such a policy would require a long-term agreement among the government, the major political parties, unions, and business. This is where leadership and coalition-making come into the picture. A program of this sort, in order to be viable in a democratic political system, requires the support of labor, and at least the acquiescence of business and the middle classes. Social democracy, as practiced in Western Europe, would provide a possible political formula for such a coalition. The problem is that, in Argentina, what is efficient is not popular: as long as Peronism, most of the Radical Party, and the left remain tied to the support of inefficient private and state capitalism, Argentina may reproduce the coalition of European social democracy (this is the design of the propounders of the "third historical movement") but not its policies. This shift could be accomplished either through a "grand coalition" between rejuvenated, realist Radical and Peronist Parties, or through the incorporation of a segment of labor into the Radical Party (an option that, in order to be conducive to the perservation of competitive politics, should not transform the Radicals into a hegemonic party). The implementation of any of these two alternatives requires enlightened leadership with a long-term horizon, a scarce commodity in Argentine politics.

Notes

1. This paper is based on a previous discussion of the prospects for democratization in Argentina. See Carlos H. Waisman, "The Transition to Democracy in Argentina: Constraints and Opportunities," *LASA Forum* (XV, 2, 1984).

2. See United Nations, Economic Commission for Latin America, *Statistical Yearbook for Latin America and the Caribbean 1984* (Santiago de Chile: ECLA, 1985), p. 146.

3. See Naciones Unidas, Comisión Económica para América Latina, "El proceso de industrializarión en la Argentina en el período 1976–1983" (Buenos Aires: CEPAL, 1984), p. 29.

4. I discuss the implications of this issue at different points in time in *The Question of Revolution and the Underdevelopment of Argentina* (Princeton: Princeton University Press, forthcoming).

5. See Seymour M. Lipset, *Political Man: the Social Bases of Politics* (Garden City: Doubleday, 1960), ch. 3; Juan J. Linz, *The Breakdown of Democratic Regimes: Crisis, Breakdown, and Re-equilibration* (Baltimore: Johns Hopkins University Press, 1978), ch. 2; Jacques Blondel, *Comparing Political Systems* (New York: Praeger, 1972), ch. 4. For more general discussions, see Bertrand Badie and Pierre Birnbaum, *The Sociology of the State* (Chicago: University

of Chicago Press, 1983); Martin Carnoy, *The State and Political Theory* (Princeton: Princeton University Press, 1984); and Jurgen Habermas, *Legitimation Crisis* (Boston: Beacon Press, 1973).

6. See the argument in Waisman, *The Question of Revolution.*

7. See the final report, Comisión Nacional sobre la Desaparición de Personas, *Nunca más* (Buenos Aires: EUDEBA, 1984).

PART TWO

Politics and Culture

6

The Culture of Fear in Civil Society

Juan E. Corradi

If we agree with Hannah Arendt's contention that "power corresponds to the human ability not just to act but to act in concert,"[1] it is clear that in Argentina the last decades have witnessed a dramatic deflation of power, accompanied by a correlative tendency to rule by sheer violence. The military regime that stepped down in 1983 went through a phase of terror, which can be characterized, also following Arendt, as a form of government "that comes into being when violence, having destroyed all power, does not abdicate but, on the contrary, remains in full control."[2] That regime depended on fear, below and above. It sought to intimidate because it was afraid of power, even the power of its friends. Although fear has become a salient political phenomenon, it has not drawn the systematic attention of the social sciences. A Social Science Research Council Seminar on the Culture of Fear, which was held in 1981–1982 tried to put the phenomenon into focus. One of the main concerns of the Seminar was to explore the ways in which politically induced fear affects the workings and institutions of civil society, especially the manner in which citizens that have become the targets of political intimidation by the state have responded—adapting or resisting—to the state's demands in the ecological and institutional settings where they lead their daily lives.

What follows is partly a report on the treatment that these concerns were given in the Seminar, taking the Argentine case as a focal point. For purposes of clarity in exposition I have organized the topics in clusters of questions, followed by a summary reconstruction of the answers that we at the Seminar provided, a discussion of the limits and inadequacies of some of those answers, and a sense of what we considered should be the next steps in research.[3] The topics discussed below represent only one aspect of the overall problematic of fear and political regimes.

I.

Assuming an understanding of the identity, organization, ideology, and tactics of "fear mongers," to what extent their irruption in government represents either a break or a continuity with deeper trends in society? The working hypothesis is that the monster did not come from nowhere, even though it became the enemy of its own society.

A great deal has been written in recent years about modern authoritarianism. More specifically, the emergence of a "new authoritarianism" in Latin America in the 60's and 70's has been analyzed in detail by political scientists,[4] and this literature has been added to the more classic studies of European authoritarian experiments. Since a coherent conceptual framework has not yet been devised to encompass this burgeoning literature, the field is marked by continuing debates. According to Fernando Henrique Cardoso,[5] the discussion on the new authoritarianism in Latin America has been centered on the following ideas:

a. A reassessment of corporatism both as a heritage of Iberian culture and as a mechanism that regulates the relations of the state.
b. The political and social implications of a new phase of economic accumulation involving further integration and internationalization of the local economies stimulate the transformation of the state.
c. In addition, the new authoritarian state is seen as a response to the challenges of a crisis brought about by a previous phase of economic development.
d. The joint operation of these pressures have led to the appearance of a type of state that is socially and politically repressive, on the one hand, and economically dynamic, on the other.
e. The economic dynamism results from the mediation of the state between the local economy and large international capital.
f. The state apparatus expands through increasing bureaucratic encroachments in the economic, political, and social areas.
g. The new tasks of the state demand the application of technocratic criteria and expertise.
h. In Brazil and the Southern Cone, the new authoritarianism has had a marked exclusionary character—sometimes leading to a recourse to terror and to the establishment of disciplinary societies.

Among the criticisms raised against the concept of bureaucratic-authoritarianism, one was of particular relevance for the Seminar, and was raised by O'Donnell himself in his initial research report.[6] It is the objection to an "*aparatista*" and "*politicista*" view of authoritarianism, and of the attendant perception of society and history from the "heights of power." Two consequences follow: 1) we should know more about the authoritarian culture and experience in many areas of social life, and 2) we should explore the experiences, values, traditions, and "learning processes" that prepare the ground for an authoritarian redefinition of the situation. In the initial discussions of the Seminar, there was general agreement on viewing Latin American society and politics from this particular angle.

II.

What allowed the establishment of terroristic regimes like the "Proceso de Reconstruccion Nacional" in Argentina (1976–1983)? Do these regimes enjoy the support of the population during significant periods? What is the basis for passive or active support of policies and practices of repression, terror, and colonization or destruction of civil society? What in civil society makes it vulnerable to these encroachments?

In their 1978–79 study on the social-psychology of fear in Argentina, Guillermo O'Donnell and Cecilia Galli asked interviewees (selected from a spectrum of classes and political persuasions) how their lives were and how they compared with their lives before the terror process. They left the definition of that "before" open. The interviewees located that "before" period in the series of events immediately preceding the coup of 1976. They described it as an intolerable situation in response to which any stern regime was acceptable. Any order is preferable to no order at all, to a feeling of primordial chaos. This quest for order prepares the ground for the acceptance of authoritarian policies. There is in fact an eagerness to adapt to the impositions of dictators.

In another paper on fear in Argentina that follows closely and comments the findings in the study cited above,[7] O'Donnell lists the social and political precedents that "prepared the ground" for the acceptance of terroristic dictatorship in Argentina. They are:

—The war of all against all—The myth of the efficacy of "purifying" violence—The acceptance of death as political currency in everyday life— The para-institutional practices spreading to many sectors of social life— Violence and authoritarianism in both centers of power and opposition groups—The vicious circle of violence, and its erosion of civil practices.[8]

In his Seminar paper, Juan Corradi referred to the circumstances that enabled the Argentine military after 1976 to reduce public discourse in that country to a simple dichotomy Friend/Foe. Similarly, Joan Dassin mentioned, in her paper on press censorship in Brazil, the dimensions and the implications of the doctrine of national security, especially General Golbery's elaboration of the concept of "total," "global," "permanent," and "apocalyptic" war directed mainly at internal enemies. Such ideology obliterates the distinctions between peace and wartime, civilians and the military, civil society and the battleground.

According to Corradi, such brutal (and ill-defined) dichotomy between friend and foe articulates a limiting type of ideological interpellation, which denies subjectivity to the Other, and turns the political antagonist into an object. By reducing them to ideological non-existence, such discourse frames them for disciplinary and exclusionary "treatment." He then described the ways in which such fateful simplification had been rendered legitimate—in other words, the ways in which significant sectors of the population accepted the drastic impoverishment of civil society. The factors can be located at the level of political institutions and at the level of social processes and values that had unfolded over an extended period of time. Corradi maintained that the devastating attack on freedoms was embedded in a larger paradigm of ideological interpellation. Like other types of ideological interpellation, the Argentine paradigm instructed political subjects to recognize what exists, what is good, and what is possible. This pattern of interpellation had also an important temporal dimension, i.e., it situated the present against the backdrop of an immediate past that should never be repeated. It amounted to a recasting of collective memory. The Present (Order) was immensely preferable to the immediate Past (Chaos). The price of maintaining Order, in turn, demanded loyalty to the regime and vigilance vis-à-vis overt and covert, actual and potential, foes. Such discourses function as a rhetoric of remembrance and avoidance. They seek to paralyze the critical will of the subjects, or, in other terms, they re-subject and re-qualify them.[9]

In a paper on the agents of repression, Patricia Fagen described vividly the dramatic nature of these processes of re-subjection and re-qualification under terror. She described how the wife of a deposed government official in Chile, trying to help her imprisoned husband after the 1973 coup, discovered that her old associations counted for little, in fact that "the former friends and associates she hoped would help her save her husband were the same people responsible for his death, and that she was as helpless and vulnerable to their power as any Chilean on the losing side." Since the establishment of a state of law in Argentina in December, testimonies like this have multiplied, giving us a glimpse of civil defenselessness under terror. Such examples illustrate the total vulnerability of civilian populations, which is the other side of the total impunity of the agents of repression (especially shocking to middle-class groups that become targets of terror), and the disappearance of buffers between the individual and the power of the state.

A second point in Corradi's paper was that the authoritarian rhetoric within which an "understanding" developed between the regime and important sectors of the population produced an ideological displacement by setting a spurious opposition between "violence and "order." The opposition masked the real affinity between these two phenomena, and hid a true sociological opposition between violence and conflict. It can be said that civil society functions normally when it is not forcefully integrated, when it provides a public space for debate and negotiation, when social messages are not "orders" and therefore require constant reinterpretation by the actors. That is a conflict society. An authoritarian society, on the other hand, develops unitary mechanisms that collapse different orders of problems, reduce the public sphere, and systematically distort and repress communication. Violence, not conflict, is the outgrowth of such a society. In short, violence and order belong to the same authoritarian equation, but they are perceived as opposite phenomena by the subjects of authoritarian regimes. This last point was illustrated by Joan Dassin in her paper on censorship:

> Censorship was designed to aid in the creation of a sanitized Brazil, cleansed of "terrorist" acts, "subversive" movements, divisions in the Armed Forces and splits in the government. It was supposed to create press images of a functioning "National Security State" enjoying an "Economic Miracle."

Maria Helena Moreira Alves's presentations made another point for Brazil. More than in Chile, Uruguay or Argentina, the Brazilian military used democratic language to in practice implant a dictatorial system. This peculiarity had, as one of its consequences, the need for military governments in Brazil to seek legitimacy based on democratic consensus through formal political representation mechanisms. The preservation of such mechanisms, even in a manipulated form, allowed some room for the opposition to maneuver. Those discursive and legal sanctuaries were smaller and more fragile in Argentina.

III.

After these regimes have run their course (very often falling victims to their own contradictions and errors, not to a groundswell of civil revulsion), what imprints have they left in society? What has been learned from the experience of fear? Is criticism accompanied by self-criticism?

Most, if not all, of the data examined during the Seminar came from the Argentinian, Brazilian, Chilean, and Uruguayan regimes—that is, from the process from 1964 until 1982 by which those countries, with different democratic traditions and in different phases of their economic evolutions, ended up subject to dictatorial and military-based political regimes. In each of these cases, the regime has looked for ways of becoming integrated into the international capitalist economy; it has increased state intervention in all spheres of social life; and it has repressed the workers and opposition groups. This, however, is where the substantive analogies end. Neither the political institutions nor the economic policies of the regimes are similar. Thus, the controlled party system and Parliament continued to function in Brazil, while the military excluded "politics" more sternly in the other three countries. While the economy was thoroughly denationalized in Chile, the state sector expanded in Brazil. While Chile and Uruguay reoriented their economies towards the primary export sector, Brazil proceeded with industrialization. Argentina, in turn, differed from the other cases in the inconsistency of its economic strategy.

These structural and processual differences affected the nature and tempo of repression, the ideological climate, the margin of maneuver for the opposition, the level of tolerance, the relative weight of the ideals of a state of law and a state of exception, and the evolution of the situation towards either "controlled liberalization" or increasing polarization and crisis. All of these conditioned the unfolding of social struggles. In the case of Brazil, and from the civil society's point of view, Alves's papers concluded that the general distrust of the system of merely label-parties under a closed regime led to an accentuated "grassrootism" and to a separation between social movements, on the one hand, and the state and parties, on the other.

Comparative analysis led us to the provisional conclusion that in Brazil one is faced with the transformation of an authoritarian order, while in Argentina, Chile, and Uruguay one is faced with the rupture of that order. In fact, one of the peculiarities of the recent Argentine redemocratization is the absence of a true transition phase (thereby increasing the risk of conflict and destabilization in the near future). This made us consider a very important related, but analytically distinct, issue, namely, the capacity of civil society to exert pressure on a regime that either embarks upon a course of controlled decompression or faces the prospect of rupture. We came to the conclusion that comparative research should focus on the organization, tradition, and culture of unions, parties, regional movements, professions, and institutions like the Catholic Church. Hugo Fruhling's paper provided detailed insight on the role of the Church and the legal profession in limiting the coercive power of the state in Chile under Pinochet. We established that more studies of this sort would allow us to gauge the capacity of civil society to break up authoritarianism and move toward political democratization.

IV.

What does it mean to live under fear? What types of personal reconstructions can people produce?

The prime instruments for researching this topic are the collection of available testimonies, interviews, and life histories. The one specific study that addresses this question is the aforementioned research carried out by Guillermo O'Donnell and Cecilia Galli in 1978–79 in Argentina.[10] According to their study, the main features of fear as a mode of adaptation are: depoliticization; a significant reduction of associational activities; the denial of evidence on abject practices (the development of a passion for ignorance among groups that are potential targets of state terror); the endorsement of economic privatization; the adoption of selfish strategies of survival, competition, speculation, in short, the blossoming of a "bad neighbor" economic policy in everyday life.[11]

The privatization generated by fear triggers a process of de-enlightenment, i.e., a regression on the part of citizens to minority status, to a sort of political infancy in quest of authority figures. For those who are not successfully resocialized, raw fear may produce the same ostensive effect. The latter can be better observed among the poor and the marginal than among middle and upper orders of society. Just as money and speculation brought Argentines physically and symbolically "closer" to the rest of the world through a sort of cosmopolitanism of consumption, fear and repression blocked and distorted communication with the rest of the world—from exiles and expatriates to democratic populations in the West. A provisional conclusion from O'Donnell's and Galli's research was that the more brutal an authoritarian regime is, the more it seems to unleash brutality in micro-settings. Public cruelty is replicated by everyday cruelty, lack of solidarity, of mercy. A reinforcement of authoritarianism then takes place in schools, work places, family, and on the streets. There is a proliferation of micro-despotisms. The erosion and collapse of institutional frameworks and mechanisms of containment of selfishness and cruelty is in turn reinforced by the controlled and saturated media. The picture that emerges is that of a "disciplinary society,"[12] that has for Gospel the teachings of free-market conservatives, and that rewards speculation, cheating and suborn. While these attitudes are enforced from above and could be said to represent a massive cultural offensive by the upper classes, they do find an echo in the middle sectors and the petty bourgeoisie. Antipopulism, technocratic and free market utopias are therefore crucial ingredients of authoritarian culture.

We examined the nature of repression in different countries. In some, we observed the workings of a centralized agency; in others, like Argentina, it was much less tidy—a sort of free market of horrors that would have made the institution of a Gestapo a progressive step forward. In the latter we discussed the specific features of a clandestine terror archipelago. The emphasis on secrecy and mystery as part of a policy of intimidation also appeared in Dassin's study of Brazilian censorship, in which she reported the preference of the military for verbal orders, psychological coercion, and veiled threats. Argentina emerged, nevertheless, as the most advanced case of secretive terror in the Southern Cone.

The culture of fear becomes very visible in a context of civil war. El Salvador and other Central American societies were mentioned during the Seminar as highly significant cases deserving careful study, although none could be produced on that occasion. Such cases are particularly relevant because in them, the cultural fragmentation produced by dependency and underdevelopment has been extreme and has, in conditions of civil war, devolved upon a culture of terror and simulation, on the one hand,[13] and a culture of "liberation," on the other. The two could be fruitfully analyzed both separately and in their interaction, and compared.[14]

V.

What was the impact of repression and abject practices on their perpetrators? What are the social-psychological effects of the criminalization of the security apparatus and government personnel? How does it relate to military socialization? How did these people digest the "dirty war"? How did boundaries between the acceptable and the unacceptable shift? What is the relationship between those at a desk and those in the field?

Patricia Weiss Fagen and Emilio Fermin Mignone provided some pertinent answers to these questions. I must here add that these questions are important in a practical sense, to guide future policies of reinstitutionalization of the armed forces. The relationship between a dirty and an open war must be explored in order to assess the changing self-definitions of the security forces. The organizations and agencies of control analyzed by Fagen were either explicitly established or, in the case of pre-existing institutions, modified "to make war, in one way or another, on citizens within their own national boundaries." This repressive design required, on the part of security personnel special social-psychological and organizational adjustments (in addition to economic investments), among them a redefinition of professional roles, ideological techniques aimed at the de-humanization of the "internal enemy," psychological and discursive strategies of distancing, etc. The repertoire of these organizational and social-psychological devices may be gleaned from the papers contributed by Fagen, Franco, and Mignone.

A study of the culture of fear would not be complete unless it explored the experienced and the projected fears of the power holders and victimizers. From reports like Timerman's,[15] and Mignone's presentation at the Seminar, it is clear that the South American officers involved in terroristic repression not only feared mass mobilization, subversion, and "communism," but that they themselves created fearful images of evil which were crucial in binding themselves as a corporate group through a special and often hallucinatory subculture.[16] The systems of violence they devised to secure social control mirrored the horror of the "subversion" they so feared, condemned, fictionalized, and mimicked. As some ethnographers have maintained, torture takes on a force of its own: "Just as the appetite comes in eating so each crime led on to fresh crimes."[17] Descriptive reports, like Mignone's, and fictionalized accounts, like Luisa Valenzuela's, concluded that step by step, terror and torture also become a culture; in Michael Taussig's words, "a set of rules, images, and meanings involving the creation of spectacles and rites which beat out a truth, sustained the solidarity of the victimizers, and allowed them to become like gods above good and evil."[18] What requires further analysis here, is the distorted mimesis between the evil attributed to the Foe by the military, and the savagery perpetrated by security forces. The "dirty war" may be seen as an apocalyptic mirror which reflects back onto the military crusaders the barbarity of their own social relations, imputed to the evil subversives.

VI.

Who was insulated from resocialization and intimidation? What processes led some to conquer fear? What explains recorded instances of heroism and courage in the public and private spheres? What type of resistance developed?

A long tradition within sociology suggests that resistance to established orders of domination—including those that seem the most terroristic—is not a sporadic or exceptional occurrence, but an everyday practice. Oftentimes, even the most spectacular successes of control are diverted and diffused by the use made of the imposed system. Subdued populations are resourceful—even though their efforts may not add up to the abolition of bondage. They frequently use the laws, practices or representations imposed on them and turn them to ends other than those designed by their masters.

Students of culture have often emphasized the capacity of the arts to convert a dominant order through metaphor, making it a function of a different register. Art remains "other" within a system which it assimilates and which assimilates it. We discussed the importance of literary production as an index of changes that take place in the lives and experience of people under fear. Luisa Valenzuela contributed some of her short stories and shared her experience as a writer in terms of these concerns. Jean Franco analyzed some recent Latin American literary texts with the purpose of gleaning from them significant shifts in the metaphors of social control and body images under authoritarian regimes. We agreed on the importance of literary production both as topic and as resource in the study of the culture of fear. Among the topics that we thought needed examination, the following stood out: The changes in genres, the relationship between official and oppositional texts, and between official and unofficial discourse, the changes in the social position of authors, the relationship between author and public, the impact of censorship, and the importance of self-censorship, the comparison of literature under conditions of internal and external exile, the different opinions among writers concerning the connection between literature and repression, the literary consequences of terror (from the shipwreck of literary generations to the universalization of regional literature through the diaspora), and finally, the implications of a "high risk" situation for the intensity of commitment to cultural activity (this last theme was introduced in a more general way—i.e., the intensity of political involvement in high-risk situations—by Albert Hirschman).

But sociology reminds us that similar processes occur in the everyday "arts of living." The obstinacy of deviance is such that it has become a field of sociology in its own right. What is sometimes termed the "degradation" or "motivational crisis" in cultural, economic, or political behavior might be seen as an aspect of the simmering revenge against power.

In her study of the impact of press censorship in Brazil, Joan Dassin described how a whole range of avoidance techniques and symbolic protests developed in the major dailies and newsweeklies. These captured "the professional and public imagination, and examples have become part of the folklore of resistance." One of the effects of censorship was the stimulation of greater inventiveness among journalists, evinced in such practices as the creative use of metaphor, and the publication of ambiguous messages hidden in rhymes or even in classified ads. These practices amount to the invention of a poetics of resistance: a cat-and-mouse game that delighted journalists, editors, and the more discriminating public. In sum, censorship, according to Dassin had an ambiguous impact: it unified the journalistic profession and created a culture of skepticism among readers. In the long run, the experience produced a broader understanding of, and appreciation for, the ideal role of a free press in a democratic society. In Hirschman's language, the relatively high "cost-tag" of independent journalism in the years of intense repression, had a long-term effect of intensifying commitment to the value of public participation. The dual effect of censorship was best captured in the conclusions drawn by Dassin:

> On the psychological level of Brazilian society, censorship did contribute in a major way to the "culture of fear" prevalent in all the Southern Cone countries. As part of the repressive apparatus that operated without seeming restraint, it helped create a pervasive climate of uncertainty and intimidation. Self-censorship on the part of both journalists and other individuals was a common result. On the other hand, resistance to arbitrary authority, self-examination, self-criticism, and re-assertion of high critical standards for journalists and artistic excellence were also by-products of censorship.

Everydayness is the order of the "in itself." It stands opposed to the order of institutions which, nevertheless, constitute the framework of everyday life. Institutions are "for themselves": they have sites, objectives, rivals, environments. They are capable of strategies. This is especially clear in the case of the state. We can approach everydayness by subtraction from the domain of strategy. What is then left? Tactics. In its most vulgar aception, tactics are ruses, trickery, dodges, bricolage. Clausewitz defined tactics as the art of the weak. Even when there are no buffers between the state and the individual, when the roots of pluralism have been torn, when institutional pressure is coordinated and severest (the extreme instance being terroristic totalitarianism), tactics cannot be discounted. They constitute the ineradicable texture of social life, Let us imagine a liminal situation: one in which action has no "proper" site, no "home base," no place except the place of an alien power, no distance, no chances of withdrawal, no possibility of self-collectedness, no "inns and resting places." Say, a total institution.[19] In this situation, there is no possibility of tactics becoming a global project, nor of their bringing the adversary within an objectifiable perspective. Still, resistance develops in a whole range of mobile actions that seize the possibilities of fleeting moments, that exploit weaknesses in surveillance, that poach in enemy territory and create surprises for and within it. Even in the thickest cultures of fear—in situations where the terroristic colonization of the life-world has advanced the farthest—the good tricks of the weak are a treasure house of inventions.[20] This is the rock bottom of hope in the human condition—not just a pious spiritual hope, but a stubborn sociological and historical fact.

Albert Hirschman called our attention to a rather surprising fact: repressive, closed societies afford an opportunity to express and signal true intensities of commitment to certain values precisely because in them all manifestations of criticism, from the mildest to the most severe, carry some "price tag" in the form of differential penalties. He recalled the experiences of Vichy France under the Nazi occupation, where individual citizens on the anti-Vichy side could give vent to their political feelings by a wide variety of actions—from telling a political joke to hiding victims of persecution to joining the maquis. The sense of excitement and of participation generated under such conditions contrasts with the boredom and feeling of powerlessness often characteristic of political life in a democracy, and of course, with the spirit of hopelessness and impotence that prevails among those who have adapted to official definitions in an authoritarian regime. Therefore, an indispensable part of the study of fear should be the examination of the processes whereby the sense of inevitability is conquered, i.e., the examination of dynamic factors in culture, social structure, and personality, that put, as Barrington Moore, Jr. has suggested, "iron in the soul." These topics can be listed in preliminary fashion:

> —Conditions that facilitate the loss of belief in the justifications of power holders. The reversal of atomization and oppressive solidarity. The creation of standards of condemnation for explaining current abuses. The emergence of cultures of solidarity that comprise opposite features to those that belong to a culture of fear: trust, representation, consent, etc. The socio-psychological components of moral autonomy. The sources of support in resisting injustice. The availability of protective "free" spaces under terroristic regimes.[21]

The list suggests that two related tasks are involved: on the one hand, the examination of macro-sociological processes, notably the study of failures, fissures, and contradictions in the sources of fear—especially state action—and on the other, the study of factors emerging from below, from minor challenges to full-fledged protest movements, with special attention to the mechanisms that insulate actors from fear and to their "recipes for coping." Both case studies and comparative analysis seem indispensable, shuttling back and forth between two levels. This strategy was followed in three papers presented in the Seminar: two by Maria Helena Moreira Alves and one by Hugo Fruhling.[22] A basic human drive pushes us to find those moments when the tables are turned and justice is restored. But behind that sentiment, our theoretical goal is to determine those conditions under which power, in Arendt's sense, is renewed.

We examined the role of resistance groups like the "Madres de la Plaza de Mayo," the significance of the definition of such opponents as "mad," the immense vacuum in which they had to operate, the creation of a symbolic space for resistance, the features of that symbolic space, the values it mobilized, the metaphors and images that were operant. We addressed such questions as: How did others react to this opposition? Was social solidarity channelled against the resisters? What are the determinants and dynamics of persecutory crowds?

VII.

The impact of change on the underlying society. Liberalization, crisis, collapse, redemocratization are all macro-processes, at the top. The question is: does civil society rise to the occasion? What helps and what impedes a creative, libertarian response to the crisis in the regimes? What are the strengths and weaknesses of civil society in the aftermath of the "great fear"? What is the impact of authoritarian and democratic traditions in society? How can we understand the maintenance and transcendence of "micro-despotisms" in civil society?

A major problem for social movements of resistance is to move from defensive to positive action, from the quest for insulated identity to meaningful collective enterprises. The main bias of most social science studies of authoritarianism in Latin America, has been to analyze the increasing power of the State and the ideology of elites—the managers of fear, the agents of repression—to the detriment of studies on the bottom of society. The experiences of the Southern Cone reveal a peculiar combination of models of permanent change through market mechanisms of the type that has been imposed on advanced capitalist societies, and the model of an authoritarian State that dominates the communist world and much of the Third World. Terror has been an integral part of this mixture. Sometimes, as was pointed out by Marcelo Cavarozzi in the Seminar, fear may go hand in hand with enthusiasm. As Argentina during the Malvinas/Falklands crisis shows, an authoritarian regime may successfully seek to induce mobilization around nationalistic, chauvinistic goals. This could be characterized as a perverse interaction between regime and society, a sort of politics of "fascist redemption."

In the face of these combined pressures, is there still room for a civil society that is more than the dream of exiles and dissidents suppressed and excluded by terroristic states or of the marginal groups that are left behind in the race for change? Is there more, in the aftermath, than the memory of ideologies that underpinned old social and political struggles? They are not easy questions to answer, but they are important ones to pose, especially as several of the societies that we have examined now face the hopes and uncertainties of redemocratization. The technocracies of authoritarian, terroristic states attempted to impose upon citizens a certain type of social life. In several cases, they succeeded only in destroying the preexisting social and moral fabric without generating viable alternatives. As their own difficulties and failures are driving them out of power, more "civil" societies may emerge. To be sure, the success of democracy depends very much on outside political and economic conditions. When outside pressures are strong and the countries feel threatened, it is difficult for democracy to consolidate itself. But internal factors are equally significant. More democratic societies will necessarily be the product of social conflicts and political processes. We must find out how, in these countries, defensive reactions from the authoritarian period can be transformed into social action within a framework of democratic institutions, and how such struggles may create a new public sphere. Will the survivors of the cultures of fear find continuity between new and old forms of protest and participation, or will they find that an age has come to an end and that certain words now mean something quite different from, if not the opposite of, what they used to mean? The period of fear has been one of great social opacity.[23] In countries like Argentina, behind often deceptive official facades, unspeakable practices took place, and around these, also in the shadows, vague movements stirred. In other cases, like Chile and Brazil—as Alves, Fagen, and Fruhling made clear—certain civil institutions assume a disproportionate role as vehicles of opposition. It is not clear how this feature will affect in the future both the internal organization of those civil institutions and their role in a more open society. Will these defensive actions, protests and demands be transformed into new social movements of the future, or will they be absorbed into the rehabilitated movements of the past? The outcome of recent political processes in the Southern Cone[24] pose certain challenging questions. They suggest that social movements today are very well aware that their struggles are about the political control of change. They know whom they are fighting against. But they find it difficult to define their constituency. They speak for a population that has been reduced to an unorganized mass. Under such circumstances, democratic candidates can be swept into office, but the issues of the role of intermediate agents in the shaping of collective action are not yet solved. Will political parties and trade unions become adequate political agents for social groups and movements in a democratic context? Will these groups and movements, instead, develop autonomously, outside institutionalized political mechanisms? And if the latter development takes place, even partially, will social action then be supportive of institutional democracy—as in the case of grassroots, local, and informal democratic experiments—or will it be perverse, shortcircuiting and blocking rather than extending and diversifying, the field of politics?

The aforementioned questions are likely to define much of the research agenda in the immediate future. In that context, we should determine the extent to which studies of the culture of fear may contribute to a more comprehensive understanding of redemocratization processes, and also what sort of studies they should be. From our own exploratory work we may glean this much: authoritarian and democratic legitimation are processes that go far beyond the scope and concern of elites and dominant classes. Therefore, a proper understanding of authoritarianism and democracy cannot be reduced to the analysis of political regimes or state apparatuses. Authoritarian regimes emerge and present themselves as a response to a preceding social and political crisis—they use fear tactics not only in the sense of intimidating the population but also in the sense of addressing themselves to existing expectations and fears. In this respect, fear mongering is a complex transaction embedded in political traditions and practices. Thus, to study the latter is to make a crucial contribution to the debate on the conditions of dictatorship and democracy. In the Seminar we strongly felt the lack of studies on popular traditions and culture. Such studies would ideally focus on these queries: 1) To what extent do traditions of popular mobilization eschew or oppose existing institutional mechanisms? 2) What are the strengths and weaknesses of democratic traditions, in terms of constituency and in terms of capacity to resolve conflicts and generate consensus? 3) To what extent and in which way have such traditions been modified under the "great fear"?

Present trends towards political liberalization and the return to a democratic regime in Argentina favor the development of field studies which were extremely difficult to design and execute only a few years ago. This is an auspicious moment to carry out field studies of microinstitutional practices as well as of more diffuse relations. Neighborhoods, local communities, and in general everyday life have become more accessible to researchers. They are natural sites for the observation of the mechanisms of social reproduction, of forms of resistance to the initiatives of central authorities, of alternative modes of social organization, of types of association, of changes in the function of traditional institutions and of the emergence of new types of solidarity in a fragmented and critical society. Such studies would allow a more thorough reconstruction of recent history than the one we could produce, indirectly and from afar.

Notes

1. Hannah Arendt, *On Violence* (San Diego: Harcourt Brace Jovanovich, 1969), p. 44.
2. Ibid., p. 53.
3. Juan E. Corradi, et al., *The Culture of Fear* (New York: Social Science Research Council, 1982), a collection of manuscripts. The papers read and discussed at the Seminar were: Patricia Weiss Fagen, "The Organized Agents of Fear, Some Notes and Comparisons"; Jean Franco, "The Behavioristic Body. The Scientific Method of Fear"; Juan E. Corradi, "The Cult of Fear"; Emilio Fermin Mignone, "Desapariciones Forzadas: Elemento Básico de una Política"; Hugo Fruhling, "Limitando la acción coercitiva del Estado. La estrategia legal de defensa de los derechos humanos en Chile"; Albert O. Hirschman, "The Frustrations of Participation in Public Life"; Luisa Valenzuela, "Selected Short Stories and Selections from *The Lizard's Tail,* a novel"; Joan Dassin, "Press Censorship and the Military State in Brazil, 1964–1978"; Maria Helena Moreira Alves, "Armed Struggle and the Rooting of the National Security State: The Second Phase of Institutionalization (1969–1973)." Maria Helena Moreira Alves, "Grassroots Organizations. Trade Unions and the Challenge to the Controlled Abertura in Brazil." Quotations of these authors, except when stated otherwise, refer to these manuscripts.
4. David Collier, ed., *The New Authoritarianism in Latin America* (Princeton, N.J.: Princeton University Press, 1979).
5. Fernando Henrique Cardoso, "The Authoritarian Regime at the Crossroads: The Case of Brazil" paper presented at a Conference on the Prospects of Democratization in the Southern Cone, Yale University, 1982.
6. Guillermo O'Donnell and Cecilia Galli, "Adaptations to Social Change at the Micro Level," report to the Social Science Research Council, 1980.
7. Guillermo O'Donnell, "La cosecha del miedo" *Nexos* 6 (1983), pp. 6–12.
8. For a longer discussion of the cultural dimensions of violence that preceded the crystallization of a culture of fear in Argentina, see Juan E. Corradi, "Argentina: A Story Behind a War" *Dissent* 29 (1982), pp. 285–293.
9. Goran Therborn, *The Ideology of Power and the Power of Ideology* (London: Verso/NLB, 1980) and Norbert Lechner, "Qué signfica hacer política?" (Santiago de Chile: FLACSO, Documento de Trabajo No. 144, 1982).
10. O'Donnell and Galli, "Adaptations to social change" (1980) and O'Donnell, "La cosecha del miedo" (1983).
11. The erosion of solidarity under circumstances of unbridled market competition, especially in the positional sphere, has been masterfully analyzed by Fred Hirsch, *Social Limits to Growth* (Cambridge, Mass.: Harvard University Press, 1976).

12. José Joaquín Brunner, *La Cultura Autoritaria en Chile* (Santiago de Chile: FLACSO, 1981).

13. Juan E. Corradi, "El Salvador: A Culture of Fear," *Dissent* 30 (1983), pp. 387–389, and Joan Didion, *Salvador* (New York: Simon and Schuster, 1983).

14. A contrast may emerge, perhaps, between the destruction of self-representative signifying practices under terror and repression, and their consolidation in rebel sanctuaries. Whereas there is mounting evidence on the impact of terror as a means for creating an ambiguous and irrational atmosphere in which there is no referent for behavior and no possibility of formulating a group identity, much less is known about the features and dynamics of the popular "culture of liberation" that develops alongside the official culture of fear.

15. Jacobo Timerman, *Prisoner Without a Name, Cell Without a Number* (New York: Knopf, 1982).

16. For an historical study of fear among dominant groups, see Jean Delumeau, *La Peur en Occident* (Paris: Fayard, 1978).

17. Roger Casement's Putumayo Report, cited by Michael Taussig, "Culture of Terror-Space of Death. Roger Casement's Putumayo Report and the Explanation of Torture" (Ann Arbor: University of Michigan, mimeo, 1982).

18. Ibid.

19. Both Erving Goffman and Michel Foucault have analyzed the mechanisms of exclusion, stigmatization, and surveillance that define a new type of despotism—a situation where proletarianization has been extended far beyond the factory.

20. For an interesting, though perhaps overoptimistic, perspective on everyday creativity, see Michel de Certeau, *L'Invention du Quotidien* (Paris: Fayard, 1981).

21. For a general and comparative discussion of these factors, see Barrington Moore, Jr., *Injustice: The Social Basis of Obedience and Revolt* (London: Macmillan, 1978).

22. Cf. Maria Helena Moreira Alves, "Grassroots Organizations" and "Armed Struggle and the Rooting of the National Security State" and Hugo Fruhling, "Limitando la accion coercitiva del Estado" in Juan E. Corradi et al., *The Culture of Fear*, 1982.

23. Oscar Oszlak, "Coerción versus información" *Clarin* (Buenos Aires), 18 October 1982, and Juan E. Corradi, "The Mode of Destruction Terror in Argentina," *Telos* 54, 1982–1983, pp. 61–76.

24. I have in mind the novel and auspicious results of general elections in Argentina, cf. Juan E. Corradi, "Two Cheers (and a Prayer) for Argentine Democracy," *Dissent*, 31 (1984), pp. 203–296.

7

Technocracy and National Identity: Attitudes Toward Economic Policy

Julie M. Taylor

I.

In today's Argentina the widespread rejection of the team responsible for the economic policy of the military regime, 1976–1981, has taken on such proportions and such coherence amongst its different expressions that it demands an explanation beyond the simple failure of an economic program. Argentines of all social levels hate the economic team in the way they hate the salient discredited figures of the armed forces, and at times the hatred directed toward former members of the Ministry of the Economy exudes an even deeper intensity.

Economic programs in Argentina have failed often but none has been the target of so much cultural attention independent of the government behind it, and no Argentine minister of the economy has received the constant vituperation that José Martínez de Hoz continues to receive. Further, ironically, events since the marginalization of the Martínez de Hoz team apparently suggest that its program contained viable elements, although frustrated in the end, while the public interprets the deteriorating economic situation as definite proof that the entire program down to its every detail was criminally mistaken.

The disproportionate hatred directed toward Martínez de Hoz and his team reveals a symbolic elaboration of economic problems that also seems disproportionate when contrasted with the relatively little attention dedicated to many political problems that contributed to the failure of the economic program, such as the structure of the central government, the failures of the leaders it produced, its internal weakness, and its growing lack of popular support. In general this study will emphasize that political economic problems derive only part of their power over people's minds from their effect on actual pocketbooks, but on another level such problems have their impact by making accessible or inaccessible the symbols of status and identity in a virtually worldwide culture of consumer values.

Thus, this work deals with the rejection of the Martínez de Hoz team as a cultural problem rather than as a purely economic or political one. The study's immediate goal is to illuminate common attitudes amongst Argentines concerning this economic program, its politics and its rhetoric, in particular. The study complements the corpus of work that gives us a macro-picture of the interaction of state policy, including the economic, and the society on which it is being imposed.[1] Investigations for the most part have described and explained politico-economic policy and the rhetoric that clothes it. The view has been consistently institutional and from the top down. But how do members of the culture, both inside and outside the government, view policy and rhetoric while living the situation these are supposed to address? What elements of a program and the propaganda promulgating it find echo—positive or negative—in the values of different groups and what form do these echoes take? Of course, answers to these questions would contribute to the anticipation of public reactions in terms of cultural beliefs and attitudes to possible future economic policies.

The attacks on Martínez de Hoz and his policy-makers have become acute periodically since my last stay in Argentina, May to August, 1983, when the team was already political dynamite. Despite the fact that I was involved in other research at the time, I could not help but take note of the wave of public opinion regarding the "equipo Martínez de Hoz." So salient an issue had this become that, near the close of my stay, I carried out some interviews to assess the potential of the theme for future investigation. These interviews and the informal commentary that had so impressed me previously have allowed me to make the present analysis, making it possible to claim that the major document used is congruent with public opinion. An in-depth investigation into the phenomenon examined here would need to be carried out through a systematic use of informants as well as of the popular press in Argentina, and would be complemented by broader politico-economic analyses over time.

At present, for a preliminary work on this complex phenomenon I will first refer briefly to the characteristics of the situation in which the phenomenon originated, what has been designated as the bureaucratic-authoritarian state.[2] I will relate values that arise in such a regime to a picture of Martínez de Hoz and the members of his ministry. At the same time, results of bureaucratic-authoritarian regimes and their inner contradictions will be points of departure to discuss how the Argentines have maintained a high level of ambivalence about foreign values, especially technocratic standards, in the face of their rejection of both. Thus this rejection is as virulent as it is problematic.

In a following section I will use a text—one that condemns that team—to identify in these pages the most important values relating to the policy in question. Using the same text I will go on in another section to discuss manifestations of the ambivalences toward these values. This will be the background against which to formulate final questions in a concluding section concerning the members of the Martínez de Hoz economic team as members themselves of the broader Argentine culture. In interviews, when directing themselves to the Argentine public, they appear to demonstrate the ambivalence noted here. However they suggest solving the resulting conflict of values differently from the man on the street in Argentina. I will underline the questions this case poses concerning cultural conflicts inherent in the introduction of universalistic technocratic values in cultures different from those that have given rise to these values. This study will propose that this cultural conflict and public reactions to the behavior it produces on the level of the economic team are important sources of the extraordinary intensity of the attacks levelled at the Martínez de Hoz team.

II.

The particular form of government that backed Martínez de Hoz, labelled by O'Donnell as the bureaucratic-authoritarian state, remains prevalent in the Southern Cone and is related to forms of authoritarian capitalist states both in and outside South America. A bureaucratic-authoritarian state maintains the subordination of some sectors of society by others through "a system of bourgeois domination supported by the expansion of the institutional system of the state which opened the way for the supremacy of transnational capital."[3] This brief definition has been elaborated in detail elsewhere (especially O'Donnell), making it necessary here most importantly to underscore two major themes that emerge from it, themes that elicit pronounced responses from the rest of society. Since responses to these regimes will be cast in different codes in each society, this investigation is limited to Argentina, although it is suggestive of areas to examine for popular response in other societies.

First, this type of totalitarian regime depicts its institutions as embodying a universally recognized rationality, allowing the government to impose impartial technical standards said to be derived from absolute standards of rationality. Second, at the same time, the very nature of the state has prepared the way for the transnationalization of the productive structure and, therefore, the "denationalization" of political and economic decision-making and of many aspects of social relations that now "extend beyond the state's capacity for control within the scope of its territorial authority."[4] Insofar as the bureaucratic-authoritarian capitalist state protects this transnationalized order, it depicts it, too, as part of the superior rationality represented by the state. As a result, as we shall see, public opinion connects the rationalism and technocracy of the government with foreign interests and values. This connection has not only been noted by analysts but has been lauded in government propaganda and denigrated as a conspiracy or a sell-out by the opposition, both popular and intellectual.[5] However, in both cases there is a marked ambivalence toward both technocracy and its supposed foreign sources.

This ambivalence toward values represented by foreign-inspired technocracy, then, is found throughout Argentina, as in other societies influenced by bureaucratic-authoritarian regimes. As such, it provides an important backdrop for the picture of Martínez de Hoz and the members of his ministry painted by the major document to be used in the present study, a special edition of a periodical directed to the mass of Argentine readers of predominantly middle class values: *La Semana*. This discussion will present the major negative values expressed in this edition and will then turn to the ambivalences towards these values, also according to *La Semana*. In particular, this investigation will probe in detail, as representative of larger trends in public opinion and popular journalism, *La Semana*'s issue of February 24, 1983, which arrived on the newsstands bearing on its black and red cover the headline "La Historia negra de los Chicago Boys argentinos," or "The Black History of the Argentine Chicago Boys."[6]

III.

The terms that Argentines used to condemn the economic team after its downfall are not new. Rather, they put into high relief elements that had been associated with the team or its program during its entire period in government. The elements that the *Historia Negra* of *La Semana* emphasizes most heavily are: monetarism; the aristocratic associations of the group; related links with foreign culture and standards, implying little knowledge of Argentine culture; and the elitism of the group in itself based on a set of technocratic values associated with world capitalism, values that therefore would supposedly contradict all that might be truly human.

In order to understand fully the definition of each of these elements that made the history of the Chicago Boys black, a context must be introduced of the process through which they went from white, or at least neutral, in the mind of the Argentine man on the street, to black, or as will be seen later, to a very dark grey. Monetarism in very broad terms could be said to be the label that large sectors of the Argentine middle class in general affixed to the policy of Martínez de Hoz. This monetarism they saw initially as a promise of plata dulce, easy and plentiful money for all, that involved more than spectacular prosperity.[7] The monetarist program held out a promise to a large part of the Argentine public—a promise of instant identity with mainstream western culture through the manipulation of classic symbols of travel and purchases of clothing and electro-domestic appliances in the exterior. Although never popular, the team represented enough ambivalent values in Argentine culture beyond its policies themselves, as will be seen below, that it was possible to think that it might be a success. "This is the history that *La Semana* attempts to tell," says the magazine. "The downfall of an empire, yes. But also the death of the last great illusion."[8]

When the dream did not realize itself, the program identified with monetarism that seemed to the middle classes in general to have failed could not be anything to them other than treason against the true identity of the Argentines on levels both national and personal. And in reaction to this negation of their identity as part of the developed western world, the Argentines defined the responsible economic team and their version of monetarism as representatives of unacceptable cultural values whose application and whose result were both invalidated. That is to say, the failure of the team and its values did not reflect the true potential of the Argentine people. The Martínez de Hoz team, then, was seen as a group of elitist, foreign [both *extranjero* and *extranjerizante*] technocrats with an equally elitist and foreign policy in their monetarism. It was alien to the Argentine world experience [*lo argentino*], and as a consequence its actions and their results could have nothing to do with Argentine identity.

La Semana proves this by opening its Black History with a full-page photograph of the department of economics of the University of Chicago, announcing, "This is the factory of Chicago Boys: The mold for Martínez de Hoz and his best boys" and identifying the photograph as "Monetarist pups." The article, through interviews with professors and students in the department, gives an impression of serious journalism at the same time that, taken in the context of the rest of the History, it repeats popular symbolic associations of monetarism, leaving unemphasized the pale and incomplete definitions offered by the academics interviewed.

Thus monetarism emerges clothed, not in its economic program, but rather in its symbolic connotations. These make explicit associations of monetarism with the University of Chicago and David Rockefeller. Implicit associations represent monetarism as part of a tutelage of the United States and a tool of the domination of monolithic world capitalism. Therefore it forms part of the unknown forces and possible plots behind appearances of national and international realities. Finally it imposes the supremacy of technocracy and of rationalization of life over human considerations. The journalist reacts, for example, by saying that "Then the cure is worse than the disease."[9] Far from defining monetarism, these connotations underline its mysterious impenetrability by the average person and its consequent relegation to a sinister technocratic elite. In this way monetarism, as a symbol, as the name "Chicago Boys" indicates, summarizes the most important further connotations surrounding the Martínez de Hoz group: firm links with aristocratic, foreign, and technocratic values.

La Semana emphasizes the concept of a native aristocracy with close links with both foreign culture and foreign commerce. This is a traditional idea in Argentina, and therefore facilitates a conceptual link between monetarism and the aristocracy. Originally, technocracy, though foreign, did not form part of the foreign culture closely associated with the Argentine upper classes. However, with increasing egalitarianism, technocratic excellence—that is, acquired by education in certain spheres— became gradually one of the justifications for the position of elite groups in much of the world. Everywhere technocratic excellence seemed to shore up high social position with functional power. Both positions, the traditional and the egalitarian, coexist, sometimes confronting one another, in Argentina's highly permeable upper classes.

They seem not only to coexist but to coalesce in the figure of David Rockefeller that emerges several times in *La Semana* to represent international high society and the power of world capital and its technocracy as well as their interrelations. Martínez de Hoz being a name equivalent in Argentina to Rockefeller in the United States, it has similar connotations in international social ties and supposedly, when these are legitimate, the same power, competence, and connections in world finance as David Rockefeller. Although an interview in *La Semana* may quote "an exceptional witness of the events" saying that the contact between Rockefeller and Martínez de Hoz was not direct, the witness goes on to admit "if somebody named Juan Pérez [the equivalent of John Smith] came by and said he would solve the problem of the cessation of payments [on the international debt], whom would you believe more? You would believe Martínez de Hoz, who raised the telephone, got through to Rockefeller and said to him, 'Hello, David. How are you?'"[10] *La Semana* makes it clear here that the confidence "naturally" deposited in a Martínez de Hoz was betrayed. His cordial greeting of Rockefeller should have been evidence of the functional contacts, knowledge and efficiency concomitant with his social position, but his eventual failure showed this to be in fact only part of a facade.

This aristocractic surname permeated the image of the team. It was impossible to escape the social position it indicated and all that this presupposed in the popular mind. "The problem with Doctor Martínez de Hoz," it was said jokingly, is that his name isn't Dr. Martínez." In the ministry itself, enemies referred to the Minister as Dr. Martínez to his back.[11] Such criticism avails itself of the negative side of the image of the upper class in Argentina. Supposedly, someone named Martínez de Hoz instead of Martínez *tout court*, would suffer from various "problems" considered characteristic of his social class. Stereotypically he would choose his colleagues through his social ties and not because of their merit or knowledge. This behavior is criticized despite the acknowledged value of exactly the same type of tie with David Rockefeller. *La Semana* quotes an ex-secretary of the economy: "He began to call on those whom he met in social gatherings. This was the way that he brought in . . . Zimmermann and Ocampo. I have no other technical explanation."[12]

Another element stressed by *La Semana* and public opinion is the lack of a knowledge of *lo argentino,* true Argentine reality as another disadvantage of a Martínez de Hoz in contrast with the mass of Martínez's. The stereotypical aristocrat and by implication his colleagues would isolate himself in his social class and his foreign-izing [*extranjerizante*] education and experience. Both this edition of *La Semana* and popular gossip identified the entire team as "upper class" by affirming amongst other things that members played either polo or rugby, both associated in the Argentine mind with the English and upper class status, implying a contrast with the sport of the popular sectors of society, soccer.[13] When, more importantly, *La Semana* quotes criticism of members of the economic team for not having lived in Argentina during several years at a time, it is important that the periodical does this in a cultural context in which referring to someone living long periods abroad may be a statement that he is doubly removed from reality: by geography and by the class whose prerogative it traditionally was to travel or live abroad. It is this double accusation that underlies the long description made by *La Semana* of the reception by Martínez de Hoz of the news that he had been named minister while he was on safari. A headline announces: "Martínez de Hoz had to stop his hunt in Africa to go to see the commanders-in-chief [of the armed forces]: Ministro!"[14] Concerning Adolfo Diz, an ex-director of a state enterprise affirmed to *La Semana* "It had been 14 years since he had set foot in

Argentina. . . . He thought that in Argentina there were Swiss and not Argentines. Diz didn't know what was 1 ATC."[15]

Finally, Argentines saw the members of this group defined as *aristocratizante* and *extranjerizante* as an exclusive group that considered itself an elite based, outsiders thought, on what was considered to be the reverence all held for the technocratic values they shared.[16] In this sense, they were seen as more elitist than the aristocratic elite itself, which at least includes human elements such as family links and cultural traditions in both senses of high culture and typically Argentine culture to form their relations.

In this image, a mini-elite excludes the rest of the world because of its imagined superior technical excellence that negates its humanity. This is summed up in the emphasis repeated in conversation and print on the group's elitist arrogance or *soberbia. La Semana* links this *soberbia* with affirmation of the group's growing esprit de corps.[17] It speaks at the same time both of the internal cohesion of the group that seemed continually stronger and of habits such as not receiving the press, that were separating the group from others whether or not this was a conscious trend on the part of the members.

La Semana describes this trend toward isolation in a negative tone, including three elements whose juxtaposition reveals the magazine's view of the nature of the values and relationships shared. These important elements are the members' imitation of each other, their asceticism and dedication to work, and the extreme security measures they took. The first of these arises from a quote taken from one of the waiters who worked in the Ministry: "many of them began to look alike . . . with the exception of Klein and Alemann, the boys [*muchachos*] began to use the same shirts as Joe, with blue and white stripes." The same waiter continues to mention the intense rhythm of work, something repeated by *La Semana* on the same page. According to the waiter, "In general, they all arrived at the Ministry at about 9 in the morning and did not leave until midnight. They generally ate in the Palace [the building lodging the Ministry], in the dining room on the fifth floor. They were very light meals because Joe had a terrible ulcer that never left him in peace. Only the second-line boys [*muchachos*] ate at Clark's [a well-known, stylish restaurant]. . . ."[18] Finishing the waiter's testimony, *La Semana* begins the next paragraph with the observation that the esprit de corps increased with the security measures taken, mentioning extreme measures taken by team members after the terrorist attempt to kill Klein by reducing his house to rubble with all six members of his family inside. An ex-bodyguard of Martínez de Hoz recounts for the magazine, "He had his car bullet-proofed at his own expense, a green Falcon with a black roof. In this he kept grenades and Itakas, and he traveled with one of his big game hunting rifles between his knees."[19]

The descriptions of these three traits of Martínez de Hoz and his "boys" share certain themes and mutually reinforce them. Not just emulation, but imitation down to the detail of the type of shirt used suggests blind, automatic copying, proving the lack of any human element of individuality or originality.[20] Similarly, the long hours of work (which might have been a virtue in another context), as mentioned here without elaboration in this particular series of criticisms, take on the aspect of the acts of automatons, of robots sacrificing any human, individual life. This idea of copying is underlined by the statement that the top members of the team ate the same meals as Martínez de Hoz even though he himself was following a diet recommended for personal medical reasons. Finally, in conjunction with these first two characteristics of the group described, the third, the security measures taken ending with those of Martínez de Hoz with their faint echo of James Bond, shows another facet of the team's lack of humanity in their total reliance on technology. Although described as objective necessities, in the specific context of these paragraphs, the dramatic security gives an impression in the text of excess, of paranoia, and thus comes to be another affirmation of the lack of normal humanity.

There is the implication of a certain element of ingenuousness in the way this blind faith in merit and technology is depicted, something of special importance in what it implies by contrast with the Argentine value placed on *viveza criolla* (native slyness). This contrast arises frequently from the kindest stereotype of the *yanqui*, the epitome of the foreign technocrat, as a type of awkward, well-intentioned but dull-witted, child [*buenudo; inocentote*]. The image of the technocratic elite, thus, ends by representing mechanical clones of their leader, disciples all of a foreign technology that excludes all elements of humanity.

IV.

La Semana, then, not only presents the Martínez de Hoz team as well as what it supposes to be its program, monetarism, as discredited by their failure, but it accounts for the failure in part by the team's associations with the Argentine upper class, foreign culture and its standards, and with the technocracy of world capitalism. Nevertheless, these associations do not constitute a definitive condemnation. They cannot: they represent ambiguous values in Argentine culture, as the pages of *La Semana* itself betray.

In the pages concerning monetarism that open *La Historia Negra* with photographs of the cradle of the theory, *La Semana* shows its ambivalence toward foreign standards quite clearly. This study has already mentioned the negative implications in the presentation of the University of Chicago as a foreign "factory" associated with a doctrine identified with the great names of world capitalism responsible for "some successes" outside South America and "three failures," Uruguay, Chile, and Argentina.[21] Ambivalence emerges after the boldface identifying the university as "the mold of Martínez de Hoz and his best boys" when a subtitle continues, "But here they scarcely know of Martínez de Hoz and his best boys," a theme which repeats in the following pages. Emphasis is placed on the one hand on "the association of ideas [of the university] with the era of Martínez de Hoz[22] and on the other hand, on statements such as, "David Rockefeller is a Chicago Boy. Martínez de Hoz is not. . . ."[23]

The nature of the upper classes as both an envied aristocracy and a rejected oligarchy emerges frequently in Argentine culture in attempts at emulation embedded in statements and acts of rejection or revolution. Even in its generally negative context, *La Semana* recognizes the status conferred by symbols both linked with the "Chicago Boys" and inextricably associated with the aristocracy, such as social connections, world travel, Martínez de Hoz's house "fronting on the Plaza San Martín," and the traditional function of arbiter of fashion in the imposition of the use of the blue and white striped shirts. For example, when *La Semana* criticizes members of the group for having spent excessive amounts of time outside of Argentina, the magazine does this in the context of a culture that puts great prestige on foreign cultures in regard to professional experience or recognition, studies, products, travels, or the very fact of living abroad. As symbols of status these are not out of the reach of other Argentines, but they are identified with the upper class.

The rejection of foreign standards as irrelevant and even harmful for Argentina coexists with the simultaneous admiration, or at least, qualified acceptance of foreign criteria and ideas. As a caption to the large photograph of the University of Chicago that opens the issue, there appears a list, with no commentary, of "The 50 Nobel Prizes of Chicago." That is to say that the Black History, which in spite of everything leaves the identity of its villains as Chicago Boys, underlines two facts that might appear, amongst others, contradictory for a popular public: an apparently prize-winning doctrine functions abroad, but not in Latin America, and a factory that has produced 50 Nobel Prize winners. The fact that amongst those fifty relatively few have been in economics is not what *La Semana* underlines. In fact, it is difficult to know exactly what *La Semana* wants consciously to emphasize, but the result is an expression of Argentine cultural ambivalence to foreign standards, in this case perhaps especially those of world capitalism. The Nobel Prize winners distinguished by the magazine demonstrate, it is understood, something concerning the excellence of the university that produced them. At the same time, the list itself, in the context of the failure of monetarism in Argentina, and the vacillation between identifying this failure with the university and dissociating it from the same, echoes another ambivalence concerning foreign standards and their relevance to Argentine reality in the eternal controversy present yearly in the Argentine mass media over the political nature of the Nobel Prize, especially in reference to the case of Jorge Luis Borges.

Monetarism figures as well in *La Semana* as representative of typical values of technocracy and international capitalism also regarded with ambivalence. The long pages of interviews with professors and students at the University of Chicago establish a tight link between monetarism and the world of science and rational calculation. Those who made up the Martínez de Hoz team held indisputably high rank in that world, as demonstrated by their "courses" and their "gold medals."[24] All of this, however, in the context of failure, insinuates that the courses, the medals and the intelligence measured by them were either irrelevant or wrong. But if merit by these standards turns out to be meaningless, the choice of members of the government by means of social ties also does not meet the approval of *La Semana*: the implication is that this choice should have been made by merit, but standards of merit are in turn also discarded as defined by and for an alien world that fabricates mechanically technical knowledge.

So the rejection of the team had to be all the more virulent insofar as it was conflictive. Alien culture and its symbols did not lose their ambiguous attraction. This applies to foreign ideas as well as goods. It is well known that in Argentine culture, as a culture dependent on different foreign politico-economic powers, foreign models have been traditionally admired. At the same time the same models can acquire strong negative connotations to the extent that they do not function for Argentines or are not accessible in Argentina. This ambivalence permeates the underlying values in the definition of the Martínez de Hoz team that these pages are examining. Each element of the accusations of failure of the team could easily in another context be interpreted as a positive value.

In the context of this level of ambivalence, the picture painted by *La Semana* attempting to resolve conflicted values must be an exaggeratedly black portrait of the "Chicago Boys." It is understood that the *soberbia,* that exclusivist arrogance, may cause the lack of explanations on the part of the team regarding their theory and action. And yet it is also understood that the same *soberbia* does not allow admissions of error and, even less, repentance in the larger frameworks of the program. The example of Martínez de Hoz is eloquent in this sense: his statement that he will not leave Argentina paints a vivid contrast with Adalbert Krieger Vasena, like Martínez de Hoz a minister of economy marginalized from power, who accepted a position with a multinational corporation. One common interpretation of this act was that his betrayal of his country was complete. The position of Martínez de Hoz and similar attitudes on the part of other members of his team inevitably introduce doubt into attempts to identify them definitively as traitors of Argentina.

And this introduces the possibility that the fault that is being attributed to the program might lie elsewhere, including in the Argentine people themselves, as implied indirectly by an example of the *soberbia* of the team cited by *La Semana,* identifying the fault in only one phrase, without source, by stating that "the epitaph for the Martínez de Hoz team could be: 'We failed because our sin was ingenuity. We didn't take into account the Argentine mentality. It requires a great deal of time to change a country of artisans into a modern nation.' "[25]

The episode, then, cannot close. Because of the ambivalences toward the culture of technocracy and the failure to admit fault, it is impossible to fix the fault in the team once and for all. At the same time it would be unacceptable to blame the entire Argentine *pueblo.* From the consequent conflict emerges a hatred that is the bitterer the more tortured it is by doubts.

V.

While the symbols associated with the economic team suggest one set of cultural problems, the actual attitudes taken by the members of the team suggest another related set of problems. These have particular interest in the context of the introduction of universalist technocratic values in cultures different from those that gave origin to these values. The team was not only seen by others as a cohesive group but acted as such, its members creating amongst themselves a mini-culture. External factors were, of course, important in the formation of this group with its own values and modes of social interaction. Examples of such external forces lie most especially in the growing public rejection of the economic program and its authors, and the physical danger that accompanied this rejection. But preliminary interviews show that the members of the team themselves saw internal factors as extremely important to their unfailing solidarity, a solidarity that they maintained once out of public office and the public view. Again, in interviews that could be no more than preliminary, they spoke of the importance to their ties to one another of the values they shared. Surprisingly, however, the values mentioned were not the technocratic canon that outsiders saw as unifying the group. Perhaps showing the same ambivalence as the Argentine public in general, members of the group spoke explicitly of the human values that united them: their personal loyalties, their family life, their shared experiences as friends. They seem to reject their technocratic image: a member of the front line of the Martínez de Hoz group spoke of his astonishment at those who passed through his office to discuss plans or problems, who, he said, invariably began with the prologue "Of course, we know that you are a man of science and statistics; therefore we have brought these tables and graphs"—which, assured the "man of science", most of the time were completely enigmatic to him and irrelevant to the solution of the problem at hand.

By contrast, when interviews turned from their professional lives to their personal lives in general, the values that emerged in lengthy conversation could be identified as technocratic or universalistic. In the interviews that were carried out, which did not include the entire team, the speakers underscored again and again, their own emphasis on excellence in their work and their admiration of the same in others; their rational plans concerning their education and future professions, to which they often subordinated personal choices and plans; the role of rational planning in forming personal relations; their dedication to public service as a value in itself. From this at first glance, the technocratic values of the team's members emerge as a reflection of the intimate values of their internal world, values that are in conflict with the "more human" persons whom they want to think that they are. These values implicitly express—explicitly team members considered such values inacceptable as a basic identity—a consciousness of being, after all, in many senses different from what they see as the typical Argentine. But all expressed marked ambivalence toward this difference which they could see as possibly stigmatizing them as members of an alternative culture, reconcilable within Argentine culture, but not always acceptable.

These problems of identity of the technocrat lead to important cultural questions. Far from being a pose, as it has been considered by part of the literature, a technocratic identity in these cases seems to be the base of the intimate world of each.[26] In the Argentine case relative to the United States, the contrast is greater between the technocratic values and those that constitute the basis for traditional relations in Argentine culture. From these cases, then, arise questions concerning the problem of a universalist, technocratic culture as an alternative and even contradictory current within a broader cultural context of more particularistic values. The social and inter- and intra-personal conflicts that are products of this situation are of central interest to the study of complex cultures, especially, of course in the context of western capitalism.

In this sense the Martínez de Hoz team has come to sum up profound doubts about Argentine identity. Something essentially Argentine may have failed: either the Argentines themselves, or a plan conceived by the best the nation had to offer, "The most intelligent. . . . Those who had the most gold medals,"[27] led by a member of the social class that, when not being vituperated, was a model and the deposit of something that could approach the ideal of "public trust." By contrast, the idea of the failure of their plan as the fault specifically of a group of sinister individuals allows Argentines to conserve the idea of Argentine culture as a value. But each time Martínez de Hoz smiles, as though his conscience were clear, or Alemann deprecates the Argentine *empresario* as at fault for economic disaster—facts reported in detail by the press— each time, doubts arise once more as to where to fix the responsibility for the failure of the Argentine economy and the related doubts concerning the Argentine identity. By cultural logic, the reaction of the public to a smile on the face of Martínez de Hoz must be a ferocious protest against any sign that might lay guilt elsewhere, thus negating the Argentine identity.

Notes

1. Fernando Henrique Cardoso and Enzo Faletto, *Dependencia y desarrollo en América Latina* (Mexico City: Siglo Veintiuno Editores, 1969). Juan Corradi, "The Politics of Silence: Discourse, Text and Social Conflict in South America," *Radical History Review*, 1978, vol 18, pp. 38–57. Guillermo O'Donnell, "Tensions in the Bureaucratic-Authoritarian State and the Question of Democracy," in *The New Authoritarianism in Latin America*, David Collier, ed. (Princeton: Princeton University Press, 1979), pp. 285–318.

2. O'Donnell, "Tensions in the Bureaucratic-Authoritarian State," pp. 285–318.

3. Ibid., p. 291.

4. Ibid.

5. Cf. Hector J. Sussmann, "Culture Ideology and Science: The Case of Argentina" in this volume.

6. *La Semana* (Buenos Aires) February 24, 1983, vol. 6, No. 324.

7. "Sweet Money" obtained in the Martínez de Hoz era through fraudulent speculation.

8. *La Semana*, p. 12.

9. Ibid., p. 8.

10. Ibid., p. 12.

11. Interview, 1983; Martínez in Spanish is nearly as common as Pérez.

12. *La Semana*, p. 14.

13. Ibid., p. 25.

14. Ibid., p. 12.

15. Channel 1 or ATC; Argentine equivalent of ABC or NBC.

16. These terms imply not only possessing aristocratic and foreign traits, but aspiring—sometimes unsuccessfully or slightly ridiculously—to more.

17. *La Semana*, p. 16.

18. Ibid.

19. Ibid.

20. See also *La Semana* (Buenos Aires) vol. 6, no. 387, pp. 26–27, 28.

21. *La Semana*, vol. 6, no. 324, p. 4.

22. Ibid., p. 9.

23. Ibid., p. 8.

24. Ibid., p. 14.

25. Ibid., p. 16.

26. George E. Marcus, *Elites: Ethnographic Issues* (Albuquerque: University of New Mexico Press), pp. 41–57, 221–256, 1983.

27. *La Semana*, vol. 6, no. 324, p. 14.

8

Culture, Ideology, and Science

Hector J. Sussmann

The troubled history of Argentine science and technology offers a striking illustration of how cultural, political and ideological factors have hindered economic development. Understanding this is important both because it provides an example of the operation, in one particular case, of mechanisms that were also at work in other sectors, and because science and technology are, in their own right, among the most important factors that contribute to development. In this note I shall argue that, in spite of the Spanish cultural heritage which included attitudes of indifference towards science and innovation, Argentina has had several favorable opportunities, which were missed because governments or the intelligentsia, or both, took decisions inspired by ideas that either were explicitly hostile to science as such, or attempted to subordinate science to partisan goals. I shall also argue that, as Argentina begins a new experiment in civilian government after the election of October 31st, 1983, a unique set of conditions exists which make a reversal of the traditional pattern possible.

The contribution of scientific and technological innovation to economic growth is notoriously difficult to quantify, but there is a nearly unanimous consensus among economists that it is one of the main, if not the main, driving factor in development. Using a neoclassical approach, based on estimating an aggregate production function in which technology is represented by a multiplicative parameter, an econometric study by Solow reached the conclusion that, for the non-farm private sector of the U.S.A. in 1909–1949, "gross output per man hour doubled over the interval with 87.5% of the increase attributable to technical change and the remaining 12.5% due to increased use of capital."[1] The results of Solow's study have been criticized by other authors, who have obtained different figures using different models. (For a survey, see Nelson.)[2] In particular, Jorgenson and Griliches claimed that, after measurement errors of various kinds are corrected, no residual to be explained by "technological innovation" is left.[3] However, these criticisms do not affect the general conclusion stated above on the importance of technological innovation. Nelson and Winter, for instance, do not use a production function at all, but take the view that "the essential forces of growth are innovation and selection, with augmentation of capital stocks more or less tied to these processes."[4] In his empirical studies on economic growth, Kuznets also reached the conclusion that growth is "based on advancing technology and the institutional and ideological adjustments that it demands."[5] Jorgenson and Griliches themselves state that their conclusion "is not that advances in knowledge are negligible, but that the accumulation of knowledge is governed by the same laws as any other product of capital accumulation."[6]

In the eighteenth and nineteenth centuries, while scientific and technical innovation thrived in the United States of America as well as in the developed nations of Europe, they were largely nonexistent in Spain and Spanish America, and this fact was perceived to be one of the causes of the economic backwardness of Spain and its colonies. The meagerness of Spain's contributions to science has long worried both native and foreign students of Spanish society and culture. An extensive body of literature, known as "the polemic about Spanish science," has analyzed this phenomenon, tried to explain it and, in a few cases, vehemently but unconvincingly denied its existence.[7] The polemic began in 1782 with an article on Spain by Masson de Morvilliers, who wrote that

> today Denmark, Sweden, Russia, even Poland, Germany, Italy, England and France, all these nations, enemies, friends, rivals, they all ardently compete to bring progress to the sciences and the arts. . . . But what about Spain? In the last two, four, six centuries, what has it done for Europe? Spain today resembles those wretched weak colonies that have a permanent need to be protected . . . the arts, the sciences, trade, are extinguished. . . . In Spain there are no mathematicians, physicists, astronomers or naturalists. Without the help of other nations they cannot even make a chair.[8]

In 1786, Juan Pablo Forner replied in the name of Spain by claiming that "the scientific glory of a nation cannot be measured by its achievements in superfluous or harmful things." He contrasted the "sophistry" of the new natural sciences with the learning in which Spain had excelled, in theology, literature and the military arts.[9]

What was true about Spain in 1782 remained largely true of both Spain and Spanish America throughout the nineteenth century. Brazilian political scientist Jaguaribe wrote in 1971 that the backwardness of Latin American science and technology is "evident today, and is firmly inserted in the historical process of those countries since the beginnings of the scientific revolution in the 17th century," and that in science and technology Latin America lags behind the developed countries as well as underdeveloped nations like India. And he stated that "during the colonial era, Latin America did not follow the rhythm of the Modern Age in science and technology because it was prevented from doing so by the characteristics of Iberian culture, which was imprisoned by a medieval traditionalist orthodoxy." However, if it was only the "medieval traditionalist orthodoxy" that prevented the development of Latin American science and technology during the colonial era, it is hard to understand why independence was not followed by an explosion of innovation and creativity. To explain this, Jaguaribe had to invoke a new reason, namely, that although "the impact of Enlightenment in Iberian culture, metropolitan as well as colonial, removed the main cultural obstacles to the absorption of modern science . . . the technological needs common in Latin America in the 19th century and the first third of the 20th remained at a modest level, relative to the time." After 1930, "technological needs" no longer were low, but now a third reason takes over: "to satisfy the demand, [the Latin American countries] had to import the totality of the required supplies, because the unexpected appearance of this demand had not previously given them the socio-economic conditions needed for the domestic production of science and technology. When these conditions were attained, however, control of the main industries of the Latin American countries had passed into the hands of foreign firms, especially from America, and so the facilities and stimuli needed for Latin America to produce by itself the scientific and technological goods needed to satisfy its demand had once again been transferred abroad, this time in a way that became irreversible."[10]

I have quoted Jaguaribe's views at length because they constitute a representative example of how the problem is often dealt with in Latin America, namely, by piling up a series of ad hoc explanations, all based on attributing Latin American misfortunes to external conditions. (First the colonial powers did not let us do it, then they let us do it but we did not do it because there was no need, then there was a need but it was too late because others had done it already, and so we did not do it either and now we are doomed.) The main conceptual problem with this type of explanation lies in the meaning of "need" and "demand" for science and technology. For instance, soon after the telephone was invented, it was introduced in Argentina, where it did so well that, according to the 1914 census, Argentina ranked second to the United States in the number of telephone lines. This certainly means that, even before the invention of the telephone, there existed a "demand" for it, in the sense that there was a large number of potential buyers. The telephone, the light bulb, the typewriter, were invented in the United States but it is hard to see in what sense the "need" or "demand" for them existed there but not in Latin America. Christopher Sholes, the inventor of the typewriter, spent six years trying to sell it, and eventually had to sell the rights to the Remington Arms Company, after his dismal failure to find buyers for his product. So Sholes was not "responding" to some predetermined need or demand, but creating a new product, hoping that people would want to pay for it, but with no assurance that they would.

The view of scientific and technical innovation that has prevailed in Latin America, and in particular in Argentina, has always been a passive one, i.e., one that fails to appreciate the creative role of the innovator. Innovation is perceived as a response to needs and to the availability of certain resources, rather than as the creation of new opportunities. J. Street, referring to the period from 1870 to 1914, concludes that "an examination of the promotive forces of Argentina's growth during the dynamic phase reveals the crucial role of borrowed technology and the remarkably passive role played by *criollo* entrepreneurship during the period."[11] How can this "passive role" be explained? I have already argued against Jaguaribe's view that there was no "need" for a more active role. A related, but slightly different explanation would be to argue that, rightly or wrongly, *criollo* entrepreneurs believed that there was no need to create new technology, since it was so much easier to borrow what was available elsewhere. Perhaps they were following the idea, expressed earlier by Alberdi, that "the very backwardness of South America is an advantage. Instead of inheriting a bad industry, South America has at her disposal the most advanced European industry of the 19th century."[12] But, if this type of reasoning really told the whole story, then one should equally well expect Latin America not to have produced, for instance, any good literature since, after all, Europe was producing plenty of it, and of excellent quality. Yet Latin Americans hold the activity of literary creation in high esteem, and don't think that, just because others have already written enough poetry and novels, it is a waste of effort to write more. By contrast, Latin Americans did not hold technological innovation in high esteem, nor did they have a high regard for the activities and skills of entrepreneurs which are needed to turn ideas into marketable products.

While in the 1880s the United States were being profoundly affected by Morgan, Rockefeller, Carnegie, Bell, Edison, Westinghouse, Tesla, to name a few, and underdeveloped Japan was inviting thousands of foreigners to teach science and engineering, and sending thousands of

Japanese abroad to study pure and applied science, medicine, agricultural science, and engineering, in prosperous Argentina the "generation of 1880" produced brilliant writers and lawyers, but few engineers. "The wealthiest [of the *estancieros* that dominated Argentine society] sent their sons . . . to the Sorbonne and to Madrid rather than to foreign institutes of agronomy, veterinary science, and engineering. Their concept of education was, as Osvaldo Sunkel has said, ornamental rather than functional."[13]

Some enlightened rulers understood the nature of the problem, and made an effort to import a few foreign scientists who would provide the impulse for the development of Argentine science. The results, however, were disappointing. Jose Babini tells, in his 1949 history of Argentine science, about the French mathematician C. Meyer, who taught mathematical physics for five years (1909–1914) to nearly empty class-rooms, and of the failure of twenty Germans hired between 1904 and 1913 to bring about changes in the Instituto del Profesorado, a normal college. There were, of course, some success stories, such as: (a) the creation, in 1871, of a national observatory in Córdoba, headed by the U.S. astronomer B.A. Gould; (b) the emergence, in the mid-1870s, of a respectable group of Argentine naturalists (such as F. Moreno, F. Ameghino and E.L. Holmberg); and (c) the creation of a well equipped Physics Institute at the University of La Plata in 1906.[14] However, the most striking feature of the period is the lack of any large-scale effort by the government as well as of any significant contribution by the private sector. While Argentina was hiring a few dozen German, Italian, French, and American scientists, much poorer Japan showed a different under-standing of what really had to be done to catch up with the more developed industrial countries. "By the mid-1970s, some 5,000 foreigners had been employed, mostly under contract to the national government, but some in private positions. The cost of salaries alone was nearly 4% of the total budget from 1868 to 1872. . . . These salaries were very large by Japanese standards, often 10 to 12 times the average earned by Japanese civil servants of equal rank."[15]

In Argentine universities, prestige was attached to law and medicine, but not to the sciences. The celebrated University Reform of 1918 did not change this, because it was based on the premise that what was wrong was that the universities were in the wrong hands, and the solution was to give control to others by, for instance, giving students a role in university government. After the Reform, it was still true that "those interested in the natural sciences—and especially the pure sci-ences—had no opportunities at all in the universities."[16] President Yrigoyen's ideas on the subject are aptly conveyed by his famous reply to U.S. President Hoover when, in 1930, they celebrated the installation of the new Buenos Aires-New York telephone line. To Hoover's words in praise of science and technology, Yrigoyen answered, in a tone reminiscent of Juan Pablo Forner, that "man's thought and sensibility are in no way grounded on [or, perhaps, one should translate "no se afirman en" as "are not asserted by"?, HJS] the progress of science but on the reality of a higher and more spiritual life, in which men are sacred to men and peoples are sacred to peoples."[17]

Yet, interest in the sciences was rising and, in the 1920s and 30s, there probably existed conditions for a scientific and technological take-off. Several scientific societies were created (Argentine Mathematical Union, 1936; Argentine Physical Association, 1944; Argentine Chemical Association, 1912; Society of Friends of Astronomy, 1929; Argentine Biological Society, 1921). Mathematics began to develop thanks to the work of Julio Rey Pastor, a Spanish mathematician who taught in Argentina since 1917. In biology, an important research institute was created in 1919 at the University of Buenos Aires by Bernardo Houssay, whose own work would earn him the 1947 Nobel Prize. But, at this crucial stage, a new obstacle emerged, in the form of nationalist ideology. In 1943, a group of scientists were fired from their university positions because they had signed a statement in favor of democracy and the cause of the Allies. Among them was Houssay, who was nevertheless able to continue his work in a private institution supported by Argentine funds and by the Rockefeller Foundation. (Houssay was reinstated in 1945, but was dismissed again shortly thereafter.) From 1943 to 1955, many university professors were fired for political reasons (e.g., for refusing to join the Peronist party), and many appointments were made on the basis of politics rather than competence. It is not that Perón was hostile to science. (At one point, he publicly announced that Argentina was about to become an atomic power, thanks to a method that had been found by an Austrian scientist that had moved to Argentina after the war, which would make it possible to have "atomic energy in bottles." However, the excitement did not last long, and the project had to be aborted.) But his main concern was with controlling the scientists and making sure that they would remain loyal to him, rather than with providing the freedom and the incentives that creative research requires. In 1952 he stated his views as follows:

When culture and science, those wonderful tools, are put to the service of good causes, and are managed by good and wise men, only then will we be able to say that culture and science play a positive, rather than a negative role for mankind. And this will not be possible or realizable until science and culture are put in the hands of the people, and only of the people.[18]

Perón's emphasis on the need to control scientists rather than give them freedom was shared by most administrations that followed him. And, in a stunning reversal of their previous views, many scientists would actually end up joining, in 1973, the anti-science and anti-freedom crowds.

From 1955 to 1966, the emigration of professionals and technicians grew to alarming proportions. (About 4,100 left in July 1961–June 1966, compared with 2,800 in July 1956–June 1961, and 1,100 in July 1950–June 1956.) During this period, Argentine universities were reorganized according to the principles of the 1918 University Reform, and in particular the principle that Universities should be completely autonomous and self-governing. There was academic freedom, and a strong effort to make appointments on the basis of merit, although many Peronist professors who had been fired in 1955 were excluded. This ended in 1966, when the military government, worried about what it considered to be the Communist danger in the universities, intervened and caused many professors to leave. In 1973, when a "popular government" was elected, control of the universities passed for a while to left-wing Peronists, who believed that the universities had to be put in the hands of "the people," and had to be made to serve the cause of "National Liberation." Xenophbic nationalism, a conspiratorial view of the world, and a purely instrumental approach to truth led students and professors to undertake a form of "cultural revolution" that aimed at subordinating all intellectual activity to the political struggle.

In the field of science, the ideology of this movement was articulated in a very influential book by O. Varsavsky, a mathematician who had been a professor at the University of Buenos Aires until 1966. Varsavsky argued that science is not "neutral", and that the idea of scientific freedom is an illusion. He provided a lengthy description of how, in the United States and Europe, scientific research was part of an engine oriented towards satisfying the needs of the capitalist system. Private and government organizations fund projects, and the scientist, although free in principle, is under all kinds of pressure to serve the system. Money also makes it necessary to quantify the value of the contributions of a scientist, which creates an obsession with publishing worthless papers. Varsavsky believed that science in the post-World War II period had failed to attain the heights of earlier years, and he attributed this to its subjection to the needs and whims of "consumer society". As an alternative, he argued that what was needed was "science to change society." The idea that only truth matters was labelled "scientism". Varsavsky did not claim that the truth of a proposition was class- or country-dependent, but he argued that its importance was. In Argentina, some things were more urgent than theoretical physics or building artificial hearts. Science had to be used to liberate the country from imperialism and to create a new society. Varsavsky did not clearly spell out how science would help in the "creation of a new society", but one can get a glimpse from his suggestion that "physicists must help the development of practical communications systems, adapted to the military strategy under study, because the expertise of engineers will not suffice to come up with the necessary innovations. The same can be said of weapons or of information-processing systems. For instance, a good problem for a theoretical physicist is how to make it difficult to discover the location of a transmitter." Varsavsky envisioned his science for social change as consisting primarily of certain areas of applied mathematics and operations research that could be used to model social phenomena. As for the new society, hardly anything was said about it except that it would be "new" and "different". All the questions about the nature of the "new" society were simply regarded as scientific problems to be studied, after the revolution, by the new science. However, the new science would certainly have to start from certain postulates whose validity was beyond doubt. For instance, one of the "scientific problems" of the new society was going to be that of "education for change," meaning "how to teach people that being 'well' dressed is not as important as participating in public life, that the prestige derived from owning an automobile is false, how to make them abandon the desire to gather money and consume, and to replace this by the goals of the new society."[19] (The possibility of allowing people to teach Varsavsky that dressing well and owning a car may be as important to them as participating in public life was to him is never discussed.)

The 1973–1974 period abounds in statements by university authorities, or by various student groups, on the need to do away with science for imperialism and the oligarchy, and to substitute science for national Liberation. Rodolfo Puiggros, Rector of the University of Buenos Aires, declared that "the fundamental goal is that the state should impose its doctrine and prevent the infiltration of ideologies that impair teaching."[20] Students and Faculty put out articles, pamphlets and books devoted to the cause of "national science," or "science for the people." To convey the flavor of this literature, I shall briefly outline the contents of one representative example, namely, an article entitled "Notes for the Construction of a National Geography," by the so called "Board of Reconstruction (Mesa de Reconstrucción) of the Geography Institute" of the University of Buenos Aires. The authors describe themselves as a group of faculty and students of geography, and the article was printed in an official university publication. Under the heading "National Geography," they claim that "there is no neutral, antiseptic, 'objective' knowledge. . . . Reality shows that every user of knowledge, be it in research, in teaching, or professionally, responds to the interests of some group." In the case of Argentina, those interests are basically polarized into two kinds, namely, "the liberal, foreign-oriented (*extranjerizante*) view, which rests on the interests of the empire and its local agents, and the national popular outlook, which rests on the interests of the people."

There follows a definition of geography as "the study of the spatial distribution of phenomena," and the statement that, in the Argentine case, geography exhibits mainly the influence of men as molders of space. And, since men do not act in isolation, but according to their ideology and the interests of their group, and in Argentina there are two interests in conflict, it turns out that "the geographic study of Argentina must be primarily historical." Next comes a comparison of different views on the nature of science, in which "irrationalism and scientism" are "unmasked" as "two vices" that follow from the "philosophical presuppositions of bourgeois science, supported by the imperialist countries." Scientism is decried because of its false pretense of objectivity, and irrationalism because "it relativizes knowledge" and denies the rationality of the real world. From all this it somehow follows that irrationalists believe in a society oriented towards private benefit as opposed to the collective good. Such belief is not only evil and irrational, but also contrary to the thoughts of General Perón, who said that "First comes the Nation, then the Movement, and only then the Men." From all this it follows that we have to fight for a new geography, and oppose the one we have learned:

> We have been taught that the United States is a country in North America with a larger area, a larger population, a superior technological development, and a larger agricultural production, that is, larger in everything. What we have not been told is that they are a pole of world geopolitical domination, that their power and their wealth were achieved by the political and economic colonization of half the world. This insipid geography that has been forced down our throats deliberately conceals the true causal relations . . . with the aim of avoiding, from the very beginning of high school, the development of a liberating awareness [*conciencia liberadora*].[21]

These ideas had practical consequences. Many professors who were guilty of "scientism" lost their jobs. Others were harassed. Working for "corporations that despoil the national economy" was made "incompatible with university teaching."[22] A generation of students was taught that pure mathematics and theoretical physics were "colonialist science." A new wave of emigration began. Contracts with foreign foundations were rescinded, and in many academic institutions the authorities cancelled subscriptions to foreign journals. And, ironically, Puiggros' logic soon was turned against his followers when, at the end of 1974, Perón turned control of the universities over to the self-declared fascists in his movement, who set out with gusto to implement the idea that "the state should impose its doctrine and prevent the infiltration of ideologies that impair teaching." In an atmosphere of physical violence and fear, many of the victimizers of 1973–1974 followed their former victims into exile.

After the 1976 military coup, massive terror was used to instill fear on, or physically eliminate, those guilty of various "subversive ideas." Entire disciplines such as sociology and psychology were suspect. Even modern mathematics came close to being prohibited, on the grounds that it uses the "Marxist" concept of vector, and denies revealed truth by declaring that one can build theories by starting from arbitrary sets of postulates. Naturally, the ranks of exiled scientists kept growing.

What little scientific research there was in the private sector was also affected by the political storms of the 1960s and 1970s. An interesting example is the research work in Electronics that began in the late 1960s in the laboratories of FATE,[23] where original ideas were pursued to design medium-size computers. After 1976, the availability of imported electronic products at artificially low prices undermined the economic basis of the project, while some of the participants simply emigrated to protect their lives.

Will the pattern of missed opportunities continue? Some facts suggest that change is a distinct possibility. The Alfonsín administration is the first one since 1930 which is both firmly committed to individual liberty and democratically elected by a majority in free elections with unrestricted participation. The ideological frenzy of the 1970s appears to have been replaced by a much calmer mood. Talk about "national unity" is common, but it is directed towards seeking agreements among various sectors rather than towards destroying the "enemy." The conciliatory mood at least guarantees that scientists are more likely than ever before to be allowed to work in peace. Moreover, Argentina has valuable resources that can be put to effective use, most notably the large community of Argentine scientists who live abroad. A renewed interest in communication with foreign research institutions seems to have taken the place of the earlier xenophobia. Some of the scientists that lived abroad are returning, carrying not only knowledge of their specialties, but also practical acquaintance with more successful instances of scientific development, such as that of Brazil. The main stumbling block remains the "passive" attitude that was alluded to earlier on, which today manifests itself in the belief that Argentina cannot invest in science and technology because it lacks capital resources and is burdened by an enormous foreign debt, combined with the view that the development of scientific research is primarily a task for the state. As this is being written public opinion in Argentina seems to be devoting most of its attention to the most pressing short-run problems such as inflation and the foreign debt. It remains to be seen whether government or the private sector will undertake an ambitious program of investing in technological innovation but, for the first time in many years, a moderate amount of optimism is justified.

Notes

1. Robert M. Solow, "Technical Change and the Aggregate Production Function," *Review of Economics and Statistics* 39 (1957), pp. 312–320.

2. R. Nelson, "Research on Productivity Growth and Productivity Differences: Dead Ends and New Departures," *Journal of Economic Literature* 19 (1981), pp. 1029–1064.

3. D. W. Jorgenson and Z. Griliches, "The Explanation of Productivity Change," *Review of Economic Studies* 34 (1967), pp. 249–283.

4. R. Nelson and S. Winter, "Neoclassical vs. Evolutionary Theories of Economic Growth: Critique and Prospectus," *Economic Journal* 84 (1974), pp. 886–905.

5. Simon Kuznets, "Modern Economic Growth: Findings and Reflections," *American Economic Review* 63 (1973), p. 247.

6. Jorgenson and Griliches, "The Explanation of Productivity Change" (1967).

7. See *La Polémica de la ciencia española,* edited by E. García Camarero (Madrid: Alianza, 1970).

8. Ibid., pp. 47–53.

9. Ibid., pp. 117–140.

10. Helio Jaguaribe, "Por qué no se ha desarrollado la ciencia en América Latina," in *El pensamiento latinoamericano en la problemática ciencia-tecnologia- dependencia,* ed. J.A. Sábato (Buenos Aires: Paidós, 1975), pp. 57–72.

11. J.H. Street, "Technological Fusion and Cultural Interdependence: the Argentine Case," in *Technological Progress in Latin America: Prospects for Overcoming Dependency,* ed. J.H. Street and D.D. James (Boulder: Westview, 1979), pp. 227–246.

12. Juan B. Alberdi, "Escritos póstumos," quoted in Albert O. Hirschman, *Latin American Issues* (New York: Twentieth Century Fund, 1961), p. 9.

13. Street, "Technological Fusion and Cultural Interdependence," p. 235.

14. José Babini, *Historia de la ciencia argentina* (Buenos Aires: Fondo de Cultura Económica, 1949), pp. 80, 88, 101.

15. T. Dixon Long, *Science Policies of Industrial Nations* (New York: Praeger, 1975), p. 139.

16. H.S. Ferns, *Argentina* (New York: Praeger, 1969), p. 147.

17. Alain Rouquié, *Radicales y desarrolistas* (Buenos Aires: Schapire, 1975), p. 20.

18. Rodolfo Puiggros, *La universidad del pueblo* (Buenos Aires: Crisis, 1974), p. 25.

19. Oscar Varsavsky, *Ciencia, política y cientificismo* (Buenos Aires: Centro Editor de América Latina, 1969), *passim.*

20. Puiggros, *La universidad del pueblo,* p. 30.

21. Mesa de Reconstrucción del Instituto de Geografía, "Apuntes para la construcción de una geografía nacional," in Universidad de Buenos Aires, *Aportes para la nueva Universidad* (Buenos Aires: Universidad de Buenos Aires, 1974), *passim.*

22. Puiggros, *La universidad del pueblo,* p. 20.

23. FATE is a large private manufacturing firm.

9

Elements for an Analysis
of Argentine Culture

Noé Jitrik

In order to begin any analysis of a possible reconstruction of what can be called the "Argentine cultural apparatus" some preliminary points must be made:

1. It is impossible to separate the political dimension from a global consideration of the cultural apparatus, understanding this dimension as the meaning itself of said apparatus and not only as an aspect that can be represented by its different manifestations.
2. It is understood that in recent years, this apparatus—in its totality and/or in part—has been seriously damaged; some of its aspects have even been destroyed.
3. It is necessary to consider, correlatively, that the process of deterioration or destruction is not the exclusive work of the military dictatorship as such but, simultaneously, of social sectors in virtue of practices and conceptions that, combined with the actions of the military dictatorship, achieve these results.
4. It is necessary, moreover, to consider the process of deterioration or destruction chronologically, in the sense that this process begins before the implantation of this last phase of the military dictatorship. One is obliged to try to understand a peculiar "situation" of the Argentine cultural apparatus, as well as its structural elements and the strategies imposed on it by a historical process that encompasses, at least, the period that began in 1945.
5. It is necessary to discard the image that could come from the expression "deterioration or destruction," that is, that before these terms could be applicable, or apparent, the Argentine cultural apparatus would have been healthy and productive, the victim,

unjustifiedly, of a set of attacks that led it to its present state of illness.

These five points express, first of all, an attitude from which to propose an analysis; from them emerge, as necessary developments, other aspects that we could consider fundamental.

1. For the "cultural apparatus" of a country one should understand the set of practices that come from a determined political process, that "comment and accompany" that apparatus, that tell of its meaning, its range and its limits, that react on it and that can, even, oppose it both going beyond the forms that it assumes in its strict sense as a political process, or closer to these forms. This first manifestation is "vanguardism," the second "regression."
2. It must be considered that the entire life of a community passes through and by means of said practices, thanks to which its members can establish reciprocal communication that allows them to understand each other, and to direct their relations with space and time in terms of finality.
3. It must be indicated that such practices are arranged in two large fields that are interrelated: that of the circulation of cultural objects and that of the production of cultural objects. (3.1) The first implies the idea of "consumption" which encompasses from pedagogical relations to those of elite culture, artistic, scientific and ritual, including those that concern the use of free time of the members of a community, the methods of "humanization" of work, the right to social information, and the forms of political interrelation. (3.2) The second implies the possibility of applying individual and group abilities to different subjects that circulate in the social space: to social experience, to symbols that guide or by which a society operates the entirety of its meaning, to the remainders of the peculiarities of a national community, to communication, etc., with the goal of producing new objects, probably unforeseeable from the point of view of the previous stock, but whose function must satisfy the above-stated principles.
4. The two fields are closely linked. What the expression a "healthy cultural apparatus" can mean is a functioning without other obstacles than access, the capacity for interpretation or enjoyment, and the philosophical and technical problems of production in both fields.
5. It must be understood that such functioning encompasses all social levels, integrating them in a continuum that constitutes the guarantee of the existence of a society that does not repress consciousness

of itself. The continuum must encompass group and individual, popular and elite culture, science and art, the University and the street, the domestic and the political.

The full functioning of a "healthy cultural apparatus" is on one hand virtual, since its tendency toward relative autonomy with respect to a political structure, in turn mediated by the play of forces, creates alternatives and blockades that engender, zones of chiaroscuro. On the other hand, it constitutes an objective from the point of view of a desirable political organization, of a class, of an alliance of classes or, simply, of a utopian thought. The analysis of the first aspect involves an historical-descriptive perspective necessary for a diagnosis; that of the second, supposes or implies an interpretation and a proposal. Without a doubt one cannot be done without the other, but not because one necessarily comes from the other but because in the description as well as in the proposal identical elements of an ideological nature play a role, since it is a question of achieving a better society through a better functioning of the cultural apparatus and not only a determined efficiency in the utilization and yield of the different aspects of culture. This perspective takes into account, especially, mechanisms of cultural consumption, cumulative or merely utilitarian, to which one can not have access through personal and social maturity. At any rate, and with the goal of producing such a description-proposal, it is necessary to consider several "conditions."

1. The cultural apparatuses of other countries, their spheres of influence, their expansive strategies, their capacity to export objects produced and their production models, their capacity or force to impose these.
2. The relation between productive capacities of their own and their own necessities of consumption and the international development of innovations or of objects of excellence. This relation is already translated as the notion of "dependence" (when there is little or no local response), or that of exchange (when the local production is apportioned with the universal).
3. The possibility of popular participation in the political process in general and, more particularly, in the decisions that order the course of the cultural apparatus.
4. The behavior of the sectors that formulate and carry out the precise cultural policies and the degree of attention that they lend to the entirety of the circumstances indicated. One sector in particular, the scientific for example, does not understand the idea of the continuum between the different levels of cultural practices,

and generally makes a separation of fields, promoting an ideology of absolute autonomy with regard to the political scope of the cultural apparatus. Correlatively, a cultural policy that disdains precision, in the highest level of consumption and production, focussing on the non-elaborative present, reproduces separation, creating conditions for dependence and weakening the degree of incidence of culture in the global political process.

5. The use of a democratic conception, in the sense of an active reciprocal respect for individual ways of life and systems of cultural production characteristic of majority and minority sectors. For democratic conception one must understand a certain institutional structure—that guarantees human rights both in its general scope as well as in the most restricted of the use of individual and group liberty—as well as an accepted system, the result of a social agreement, in which a community recognizes itself, and whose use impedes the violation of the norms that rule said structure.

Taking into account all these factors one could begin a concrete analysis that would allow one to surmise the viability of a reconstruction of the Argentine cultural apparatus, with the supposition that an analysis of this type could give rise to a program, linked, in an explicit and assumed way, to a democratic political initiative with an ethical content, that renounces the complicities and crimes of the recent past.

It is evident that the system of disappearances, kidnappings, assassinations, legal and clandestine imprisonments and tortures—organized systematically with deliberation and cruelty, on a philosophy of the extermination of the enemy—has unsettled Argentine society, traumitizing it to the point of exhaustion or, at least, has discouraged confidence in a capacity of cultural production as we conceive of it here. On the contrary, it has stimulated a disproportionate and unproductive consumption more of "forms of life" than of culturally valuable objects (the reign of household electrical appliances in opposition to the almost complete elimination of the publishing houses).

To the extent that that terror has been directed against political activists and workers and intellectuals, it has also damaged the critical capacity of society as a whole, which, to the same degree, has been led to a form of cultural existence based on countervalues such as repression, self-censorship, vigilance, the acceptance of a subordinate and secondary scheme of values (an evident lack of equilibrium: the importance that soccer has had as escape or promoted compensation in the period versus the deliberate languishment of a University reduced to routine and control).

This form of genocide began in the recent past, with the formation of parapolice groups in the epoch of Perón and Isabel Perón. Exercising a system of control through terror, they initiated the restriction of spontaneous forms of political and social grouping, of free expression of ideas, of the structures of mass demonstrations (marches and assemblies), of struggles for renovation in trade unions, of neighborhood life, etc. They interfered equally in university and editorial life, as well as in friendly and family relations, to the degree to which they created conditions of secrecy, which seems to be the only refuge in which it is possible to continue life apart from terror although, logically, determined by it. Finally, they expelled culturally productive sectors that have no way of defending themselves from aggression and that, before accepting the prospect of an agreement with the enemy or of paralysis, preferred exile. Certainly, these traits are readopted and articulated to perfection by the military dictatorship after the coup of 1976.

This depressive system is accentuated by the economic crisis that accompanied the scheme of repression: it seems to support a project of the country that, at least, must adjust to an international situation which it cannot influence and on which it must depend, neutralizing all its capabilities.

It is evident that, in the beginning, the enlightened sectors of the dominant classes—who, in a classic sense of interpretation seem to have delegated power to the military—took pleasure in this turn of events. They did not notice, or did not want to notice—for convenience more than for lack of enlightenment—the consequences that this rearrangement could entail. The exile of intellectuals, for example, did not disturb them; editorial censorship did not provoke a shudder in them and, even less, any condemnation; the disappearance of people or the correlative appearance of movements such as that of the Mothers of the Plaza de Mayo, provoked aggressive indifference in them. In general, the intellectual recession was only important to them insofar as it affected or could affect certain advantages in social status.

Something similar happened with the political parties that left aside these topics to take refuge in the purely technical aspects of their survival as structures, to such a degree that they excluded from their formulations not only the ethical side of the question but also any thought about the future of a country so seriously affected by this process of violent "reordering" of society.

A relation can be established between the suffocation of which the University and the scientific and intellectual universe in general have been victims and the repeated dismantlement of structures and human resources that has been taking place for years. Except in rare moments, little has been done to detain the emigration of scientists that on impoverishing our apparatus enrich others, in which they find acceptance and understanding, in general in centers linked to rich countries. In those cases the problem is eliminated with sarcasm; however, developing nations also offer these opportunities. In one form or another a paradox occurs: we expel mental capacity to later buy what that capacity produces in other places. This behavior is not easy to explain: the classes in power disdain, because of their fear of the relative autonomy of the cultural apparatus and its effects, the corresponding relative subjection that this apparatus always maintains with the State and, to its misfortune, with society as a whole.

To resolve this problem historically the following policies have been adopted: 1) to incline the balance toward the technical, drowning theory; 2) to lighten the strictly academic requirements; 3) to suffocate political life with the goal of avoiding future problems; 4) to adopt demagogic measures related to aspects of social and economic pressure of the cultural institution; 5) to return to purely professionalist criteria that consolidate feelings and privileges of class. These policies, adopted as alternatives, have consolidated the crisis and have made it chronic so that when dictatorship arrived its policy in the matter crowned a process and made it culminate.

Perhaps this explains why the social sciences have not developed in their most modern form, which began to emerge as a necessity of the country in the University of 1956, in a manner analogous to that recorded in other countries. Equally, perhaps this explains why the exact sciences have declined both in the abundance of scientists and in the quantity and quality of their contributions and, also, why doctors and lawyers again have political importance in the cultural apparatus.

Surely, the budgets of education and culture, public health and armed forces have followed opposite lines for many years now: the first two down and decreasing, the last up and increasing. This indicates that the state has continued to conceive of itself more in a military sense than a civilian one, a process that has not been pointed out with the necessary rigor and awareness, perhaps because of political reasons of obedience or submission to the more and more powerful gendarmes. However, perhaps the defeat suffered in the Malvinas is making an examination of this type appear, without concessions or with less concessions to armed power. In addition to having diverted the best resources of a country, impoverishing it, the military has consummated its work bringing death to many of its youth. They have made it clear, also, that, except to threaten civilian society and repress it, the brutal exploitation of national labor did them no good. This budgetary tendency starts in the moment in which the military begins to conspire and to overthrow civilian governments that, however, never limited them, as if in surrendering their common wealth to them, they could insure their subjection to legality.

Notes

Translated by Carolyn A. Morrissey.

About the Contributors

Juan E. Corradi is associate professor of sociology at New York University. His publications include *Ideology and Social Change in Latin America* and *The Fitful Republic: Economy, Society, and Politics in Argentina.*

Noé Jitrik is professor of literature at the Autonomous University of Mexico. He is the author of *El mundo del ochenta, Muerte y resurrección de Facundo, Las armas y las razones,* and several other books.

Michael Monteón is associate professor of history at the University of California, San Diego. His publications include *Chile in the Nitrate Era: the Evolution of Economic Dependence, 1880–1930* and papers on Latin American economic history.

Monica Peralta-Ramos is currently in charge of academic affairs at the Argentine Embassy in Washington, D.C. She is the author of *Etapas de acumulación y alianzas de clases (1930–1970)* and *Acumulación del capital y crisis política en Argentina (1930–1974).*

David Rock is professor of history at the University of California, Santa Barbara. His publications include *Politics in Argentina, 1890–1930: the Rise and Fall of Radicalism* and *Argentina 1516–1982: From Spanish Colonization to the Falklands War.*

Hector J. Sussmann is professor of mathematics at Rutgers University. He has published more than 80 papers on theory of control, mathematical modelling, and the philosophy and methodology of science.

Julie M. Taylor is associate professor of anthropology at Rice University. She is the author of *Eva Perón: The Myths of a Woman* and other works.

Juan M. Villarreal is professor at the Latinoamerican Faculty of Social Sciences (FLACSO), Buenos Aires. His publications include *El capitalismo dependiente: Estudio sobre la estructura de clases en la Argentina.*

Carlos H. Waisman is associate professor of sociology at the University of California, San Diego. He is the author of *Modernization and the Working Class: The Politics of Legitimacy* and *The Question of Revolution and the Reversal of Development in Argentina* (forthcoming).

Index